INTO THE SUN

INTO THE SUN

Claude Thompson

Acknowledgements

I wish to acknowledge the support of family and friends in bringing this book to publication. In particular, it is important to me to specifically acknowledge the contributions of the late A.R.D. Fairburn for his poetry, and Sid Scales for permission to include his cartoons used in this book.

First published 1996
by the author
PO Box 343, Warkworth, New Zealand

ISBN 0 9583498 1 9

Designed by Suellen Allen
Production by Pages Literary Pursuits
Printed by SRM Production Services, Malaysia

Contents

Preface

In March 1942 I was captured in Java and for the next three and a half years was a Japanese Prisoner of War. During that time I was in over twenty camps and travelled well over 3000 miles in Japanese luxury ships (although under indescribable conditions), as well as on long train and truck journeys, and by a lot of foot slogging. I think I had probably been further, and stayed in more camps, than almost any other prisoner of war in that region.

This travel gave me only glimpses of places that looked very beautiful, and I met many Indonesian people and liked them a great deal. Some Indonesian soldiers were also POWs; I talked often with them and spent a great amount of my spare time trying to learn their language and finding out how they lived when at home.

Eventually, after the war, I returned home to New Zealand, and gradually got back to reasonably good health, but I always had a great desire to return to Indonesia and confirm my impressions — were those islands which I had visited as beautiful as I imagined, and were the people so interesting?

It is one thing to want to travel, but another to be able to do it, especially as I have a wife and four children. When I was about 60 years of age I sometimes thought of retirement, but never quite got to the point of either retiring, or returning to Indonesia. Then, at Christmas 1971, fate took a hand. A very great friend, almost exactly my own age, died suddenly from a heart attack. One of those at his funeral, younger than ourselves, also died suddenly within a few weeks. A month later, two more were dead. That decided me. Acting quickly, I sold my business and asked my wife Betty if she would like to go overseas and look at some of my old prisoner of war camps, which I remembered as places of great misery and difficulty, but also as having great natural beauty. I thought that Betty would have reservations, but she was surprisingly keen.

At first we decided to go by sea, travelling on a small ship from Sydney to Singapore. However, a great sense of urgency possessed me, and we booked to fly direct to Singapore from Auckland with only two short stops at Melbourne and Perth. Thank God we did this, for if we had delayed our departure by three days we would have had knowledge of the failure of a very large company which, being a tenant of mine, was a major source of my income. Had we known of this failure we most certainly would not have gone. As it was, I knew nothing of all this until our return from Indonesia.

In Singapore we stayed at the Raffles Hotel. Our Chinese friends took charge of us and we had a wonderful time. Dominating my thoughts, however, was my desire to get to Pekan Baru, a town in the middle of Sumatra, situated on the south bank of the Siak River about 100 miles from the sea, and approximately thirty miles above the equator. The only way to get to Pekan Baru was by boat or aircraft. There was no road. Our tickets had been bought in New Zealand but were open dated. Our New Zealand travel agent told us to go to a certain Singapore travel agent and ask for Sammy — he would fix our travel arrangements to Pekan Baru.

But it wasn't quite so easy. When we asked for Sammy he said that such a journey was impossible, and that the only plane that flew to Pekan Baru was Indonesian, also that the Indonesian oil company block booked all seating on that plane. Seeing how important it was for us to go, Sammy again rang the airline, but again came the answer — "Impossible". But he had another suggestion — that we try another oil company which had an office in Singapore. Perhaps they could help. We called the office and this time asked for the manager. We were introduced to an American, Earl Sanders, and explained our problem to him. "Pekan Baru?" he exclaimed. "What the hell for? It's an awful dump!" "It's a sentimental journey," I said. "I helped build a railway line from Pekan Baru to Padang."

"Bullshit!" he replied. "There's never been a railway at Pekan Baru. I've been there lots of times."

"Oh yes, there was," I said. "And thousands of native labourers, and thousands of prisoners of war died there. Some of them were Americans," I added.

"Well, I've never heard of any railway," he repeated. But although I don't think he was entirely convinced, he said he was sure he could get us seats on the plane, but it could take some time because he would have to write to Djakarta.

Earl Sanders was as good as his word. It was not long after this that we boarded a Fokker Friendship and flew from Singapore, over a maze of islands, and then for miles and miles over tall, continuous rainforest. There was not one clearing to be seen — only forest, divided by the yellow Siak River. When we landed at Pekan Baru we were entering Indonesia. From all we had heard Customs here could be difficult and we

Siak River, Pekan Baru, 1972

TOP: The author and his wife surrounded by children, Pekan Baru, 1972.

ABOVE: The author with an old man (left) who worked on the railway line. As a ten-year-old the man on the right of the picture traded clothes under the wire at Camp 1.

felt very nervous as we waited in the long queue.

Then a well dressed Indonesian approached and asked if we were Mr and Mrs Thompson from New Zealand. When we said yes, he picked up two of our bags and asked us to follow him straight through Customs, to a shining black car which was waiting outside.

"My name is Evan. I am the Public Relations Officer for the oil company," he said and diffidently presented us with an itinerary of what the oil company had arranged for our visit. For the first time we were VIPs. The first stop on the itinerary was lunch. Evan told us that he and his wife would be there with us, as well as his boss who was flying from Djakarta with his wife especially for the occasion. All four Indonesians spoke perfect English, and were very well informed. I tried out my Malay, to their great amusement, but they encouraged me to continue. The food was Ristaffel, and was wonderful — the best Indonesian food I had ever had.

It was about halfway through the luncheon that the Public Relations Officer dropped his bombshell.

"Mr Thompson," he said. "Since Mr Sanders of Caltex Asia told us that two New Zealanders were coming to find an old railway we have made energetic and extensive enquiries amongst our large staff, and up to this moment we have not found any evidence whatsoever that a railway was ever built from Pekan Baru." I did not enjoy the rest of my lunch. My mind leaped back to my arrival at Pekan Baru over 27 years before.

I remembered the panic and brutality of the Japanese as we were hustled off the boat. They seemed to go mad whenever we were moved from one place to another, and with cries of "Speedo! Speedo!" they beat us with rifle butts to try to get us moving when it was impossible because of the crowding. I remembered seeing the great piles of sleepers and rails everywhere, and some POWs working. We were herded into diesel trucks which ran along the rails, and taken to the banks of a large river with steep banks. Here we were made to walk across the sleepers which were loosely strewn across the main girders of the bridge that spanned the river. The drop below was frightening, but the Japanese were even more terrifying and fear got us all across. After a long tiring walk in the darkness we eventually came to Camp 5, a weird sight, with lots of fires from the cookhouse, plus the fire that was kept going in the guard house because the Japanese were afraid of being taken by tigers.

I remembered the squalor and the misery, the dysentery, the beri beri and malaria from which so many had suffered. And the hellish conditions at Haruku, the worst camp of all.

And I remembered my last days as a Japanese prisoner of war, how very hectic and terribly exciting they were, and how, on that day of days when it was all over, I stood at the aerodrome at Pekan Baru, naked except for a piece of sacking, and greeted Lady Mountbatten as she arrived in Sumatra.

I thought of all this, but could remember no town. I knew there must have been one close by, but I had not seen it. How would I prove that a railway was ever made when the local people did not know of it?

When the luncheon was over the Public Relations Officer took Betty and me down to the wharf.

"Do you remember anything?" he asked me.

"No," I said, "I have not been here before."

He then said that there was an old wharf further down the river. By this time about fifty or sixty children had crowded around us. They were bright, healthy looking kids. When we drove slowly over the bumpy track they followed us. At the second wharf Evan asked me again whether I recognised anything. Again I had to say no.

"Well, that's it," he said. Then he suddenly remembered another old derelict landing, still further down the river. When we got there, still followed by the children, I looked about.

"I don't recognise anything," I said to Evan, "but I have a queer feeling of having been here before."

At this, Evan called the children around him and asked if any one of them had seen any part of a railway line ... a wheel? ... a track? ... an engine? When he said "engine" a boy put up his hand and said "I have". Evan spoke quickly to him. Then he turned and said, "This boy says there is an engine in his garden."

With the boy sitting on the bonnet of the car we turned away from the river and drove a narrow track for about four hundred yards. There, beside a small school, was a very old steam locomotive, with a banana palm and tapioca plants growing around it.

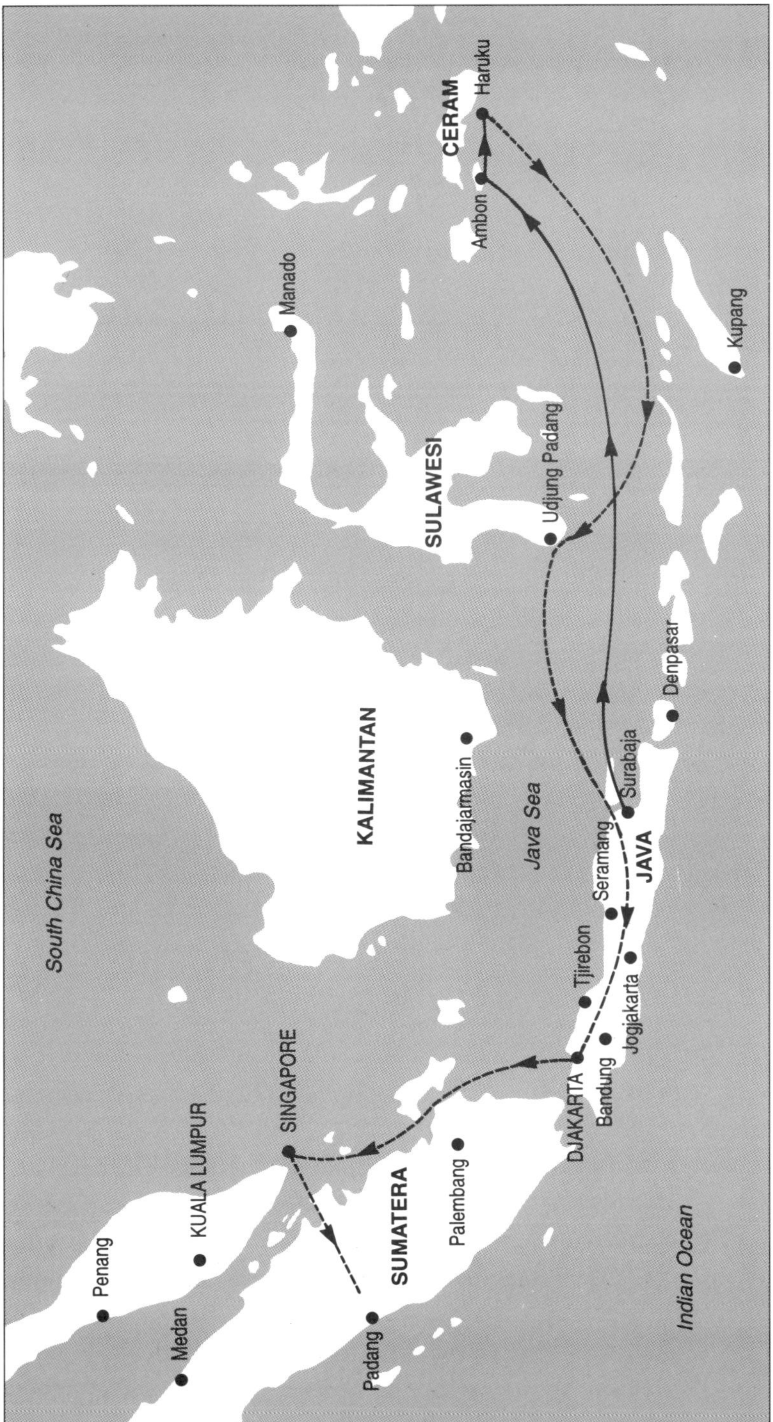

Journey to and from Haruku.

Chapter 1

SINGAPORE

In the tropics the change from day to night is sudden and very spec tacular — too wonderful to miss and well worth the effort of getting outside. In a few minutes it would be time. I struggled out and sat on the seat fixed to the hut.

Ceram Island, in the Moluccas, was dark green and brooding, its peaks mirrored in the still sea. Scarcely a rustle came from the coconut palms overhead. The only movement or sound on the clean sandy beach was the regular lap of inch-high waves. As I watched from my seat Ceram changed colour with the sunset. The sea caught fire. This glorious sight was as good as food — or almost. The grove of nutmegs in which the camp was built darkened. A feeble cry of pain brought me back to earth. I struggled up to get inside. Food would soon be served.

Before I reached the entrance the stench was like a wall. It was the stench of rotting flesh and death. A few smoking coconut oil lamps gave a pale light as I shuffled to my sleeping space. While I had been out to watch the sunset the man in the space next to mine had died. They were carrying him away. But the big question was, would his ration of food come? If it did — half for me and half for Fred. That was the rule.

* * *

That story really began in April 1941 at Woodbourne Aerodrome, Marlborough, in the South Island of New Zealand. We had finished our flying training and had been told our postings. I had to go to the Far East, Singapore — an area, they said, where there was not much chance of war. That evening the officers of the station gave us a send-off party in their mess. The CO wished me luck. He said I was fortunate to be going to Singapore because there they had the most up-to-date aircraft, and it would be England afterwards, probably. In Singapore I flew obsolete Vildebeests, one of the oldest service aircraft used during the last war. Even of these there were very few. And afterwards, it was not England.

On our way to Singapore we stopped for about a week in Java. The British community in this country welcomed us royally and we were showered with kindness. For about five days the 24 pilots of our party were entertained in Soebang, the headquarters of the huge Anglo-Dutch Plantation Company. Here we were treated to a standard of living that was to us almost unbelievably luxurious. If we played snooker or billiards in the club, we had our Javanese boys to chalk our cues or hand us the jigger. A boy kept the score and another was always in attendance with whisky-sodas and cigars. If we played golf we had only to try hit the ball. The native caddies teed up, carried the clubs and found the balls for us.

During this period I stayed with the supervisor of the company's tea estates, a Mr. Masefield, who was a relative of the Poet Laureate. It was his job to look after from 20–30,000 acres of tea, dozens of factories and the research work done on or in them. Other men supervised the other activities of this enormous company, which had about 30,000 acres of rubber, the same area of rice, about 25,000 acres each of tapioca, sisal, teak forest and quinine. During my stay these kind people put at my disposal a huge shiny Straight Eight Buick, complete with driver. All too soon we had to say goodbye.

We sailed into Singapore feeling very important. We were going to start work and really learn to fly the big ones — the up-to-date aircraft the CO had told us about. We expected a small reception committee on the docks. No one was there. After a number of telephone calls and a long, long wait, the authorities decided that they had better do something about us. It was our first experience of the Great Apathy in Malaya. The first Malay words we were to learn were "Tida Apaapa" — "Why worry?"

At first I was sent to 205 Squadron. Here I was to learn how to handle flying boats. The Squadron was equipped with Catalinas, and we had a most interesting course which included seamanship. Unfortunately, I was not here for long as the extra Cats that were to arrive did not turn up and I was transferred to the pigs — Vildebeests in 100 Squadron.

During February 1942 we had to leave Singapore. Our aerodrome was untenable. It was being bombed continuously and finally was shelled from across the Johore Strait. The bombing by the Japs was deadly and accurate. Perfect formations of either 27 or 54 planes attacked at about 17,000 feet. At some given signal all of the planes dropped a stick of bombs and systematically destroyed hangars, workshops and the drome.

On our way to Singapore the Dutch had welcomed us with open arms,

ABOVE: Anglo-Dutch Plantation Company supervisor Mr Masefield and his wife in front of their mansion.

LEFT: Tea being harvested on the estate in Soebang.

RIGHT ABOVE: Javanese boys covered with tapioca, which when first manufactured is a very fine powder.

RIGHT: Sacks of tapioca in a factory at Soebang.

but when we left and came to Java it was a different story. They hated us because we had not held on to Singapore. They held us personally responsible. It was obvious by this time that Singapore would fall, and it would soon be Java's turn to be attacked by the Japanese.

At Palembang as we passed through, I noticed the huge oil pipes on the river bank and remarked that all the Dutch had to do to stop the enemy getting up the river would be to let out oil on the ebb tide and set fire to it. This was never done, and the enemy came unhindered up the river. They also dropped paratroops at Palembang.

In Java our squadron and 36 Squadron combined and we operated about nine planes which took part in the Battle of the Java Sea. Eventually, at the beginning of March we went to an aerodrome at Tasikmalaya, on the south-east coast of Java. Only five planes remained, three serviceable. With these we flew at night and bombed Kalijati Aerodrome, for by now the enemy were in Java.

Kalijati Aerodrome was a very large Dutch Air Force establishment. From it the R.A.F. and the R.A.A.F. were operating. After the enemy landed in Java the Dutch never bothered to notify this very important station and the Japanese made their way on motorcycles and light trucks for about 40 miles and surprised the camp. The first warning the camp had was the noise of them on their motorcycles gunning the aerodrome. It is greatly to the credit of the aircrews that so many planes were started up and flown off in the confusion. We were ordered the following day to treat Blenheim aircraft as unfriendly. A week later two of our three Vildebeestes were left and they flew off toward Sumatra. Aircrew who had wives in India had been given the chance to escape in this way. These old kites had a range of only 300 to 400 miles. This would take them a little way up the west coast of Sumatra, hundreds of miles from India. If the crew saw a friendly ship they were to land in the sea beside it, or fly until their petrol was exhausted and land in the sea as close as possible to shore. A landing on a beach was considered too dangerous because of soft sand. Once on land they were to look for some sort of craft and try to get to Ceylon or India.

We who were left, about ten aircrew and 150 ground staff, decided to go up to the hills to fight. All day on March 7 we sorted out the gear we would use and destroyed whatever might have been useful to the invaders. It seemed desecration to destroy my parachute. I saved the cords and most of the silk. We were issued with .303 rifles and ammunition, and on March 8 set off in convoy for the hills. We did not get far. At Garoet —

about 20 miles from our drome at Tasikmalaya — we were stopped by an army of Dutch and made to stack our arms and proceed with them to a camp and await the Japanese. Most of us threw away the bolts of our rifles. This made the Dutch very angry indeed.

The Dutch took us to a small place called, I think, Ttikadjang. All along our route the Dutch were wearing white armbands and waving white flags. We slept that night in a loft of a tea factory; I remember the fragrance of tea was very pleasant. In the morning we moved to a place called Pamagaten — a further 5–6 miles — and there we stayed in another tea factory. It was very restful during our stay at Pamagaten. A reaction set in after the months of fighting and we were content to sleep and eat. We did this for about three days. We saw no Japanese. The Dutch gave all the orders.

Our next move was a short one but it took us into lonely, high country, most of it planted in tea. Our camp was a cluster of old buildings — a drying shed, a broken-down bungalow and a few open sheds. We were told that we were to stay here for the duration, and that we should plant gardens and make ourselves comfortable. It seemed to me almost a pleasant prospect. Here we could make ourselves snug, grow enough food to live on, and enjoy the really delightful surroundings. I think a tea garden is one of the loveliest places on earth and I felt sure I could exist in this one for the short time we would be prisoners. We were all sure the Americans would take Java in about three months.

In the camp I was made No.1 Public Works. Our first job was a bathing pool: we dammed our small stream and made a fairly deep pool. The next job was a water supply for the camp. We had seen how the natives carried water great distances by using bamboo as pipes so we got started on the same idea, and I was kept very interested during the daytime.

But at night I wondered if it were possible to escape from Java. Escape from the camp would have been easy, but not to escape from Java. In Java, a country with about 42 million people, nearly all dark skinned, a fugitive white was as noticeable as a black sheep in a flock. Some of our men had tried to get away on the first day and had driven down to the coast. They had always come back and reported: "Not a chance."

All of my experience of the coasts about these parts had been of the sheltered coasts of Malaya, the east coast of Sumatra and the north of Java. I felt sure, optimistically, that the south Java coast would be the same and I would be able to find a boat of some kind and make my way to Sumatra, and from there in a larger boat to Ceylon. I still had some maps and a small compass, but I wanted a cobber. I mentioned it to some of the boys, but they said: "Hopeless." But a few days later, on March 19, we had bad news. The camp was to move and we had to march to some new destination. I made up my mind that escape was now or never for me.

Chapter 2

DOWN TO THE COAST

I put my escape proposition to a young Scot, Eddie, who seemed to have plenty of guts, and he agreed to come with me. Our plan was to live in the jungle beside the camp for a few days, so we got together a lot of gear to make ourselves as comfortable as possible. I had my waterproof flying suit and its warm, padded inner suit, which would do as a sleeping bag. Our dress was shorts and shirt, long socks and boots. I had an Australian fur felt hat, and Eddie had a peaked cap. In my pack I had (besides the flying suit) a large quantity of parachute silk, about a dozen tins of food, some loose porridge meal, tea and condensed milk, a small stove and can of petrol, compass, maps and charts, about 100 guilders in Dutch money, and a change of shirt, socks, shorts and underwear. The packs were far too heavy, but we decided we would easily get rid of the gear when we started to march. When we left camp I had a parang — a large knife — but no firearms. Later we got an automatic pistol from some soldiers we met down the coast.

Before leaving camp I hid my cameras in a partition of the wall of one of the huts. I wrapped in parachute silk a Super Ikonta with a Zeiss 2.5 lens, a Kodak 3.5 lens, a Kodak cinecamera, two exposure meters and two electric razors.

That night, laden with all our gear, we left camp and hid in a large patch of jungle nearby. We decided it would be a good thing to hide up for a few days and then move southwards to the coast, a distance of about 30 miles, but after one day and night we had had enough and were keen to get away. The first day waiting in the jungle was indescribably long. We started at the slightest noise. The next night was not much better though we did get some sleep.

In the morning we cut our packs down to a minimum and were having a last meal when a slight noise made us look around. There were natives eyeing us. We thought: "This is it; they want to hand us over." But no, they were completely friendly and, when we had given them the gear we were abandoning, more than friendly. They offered to guide us to a nearby

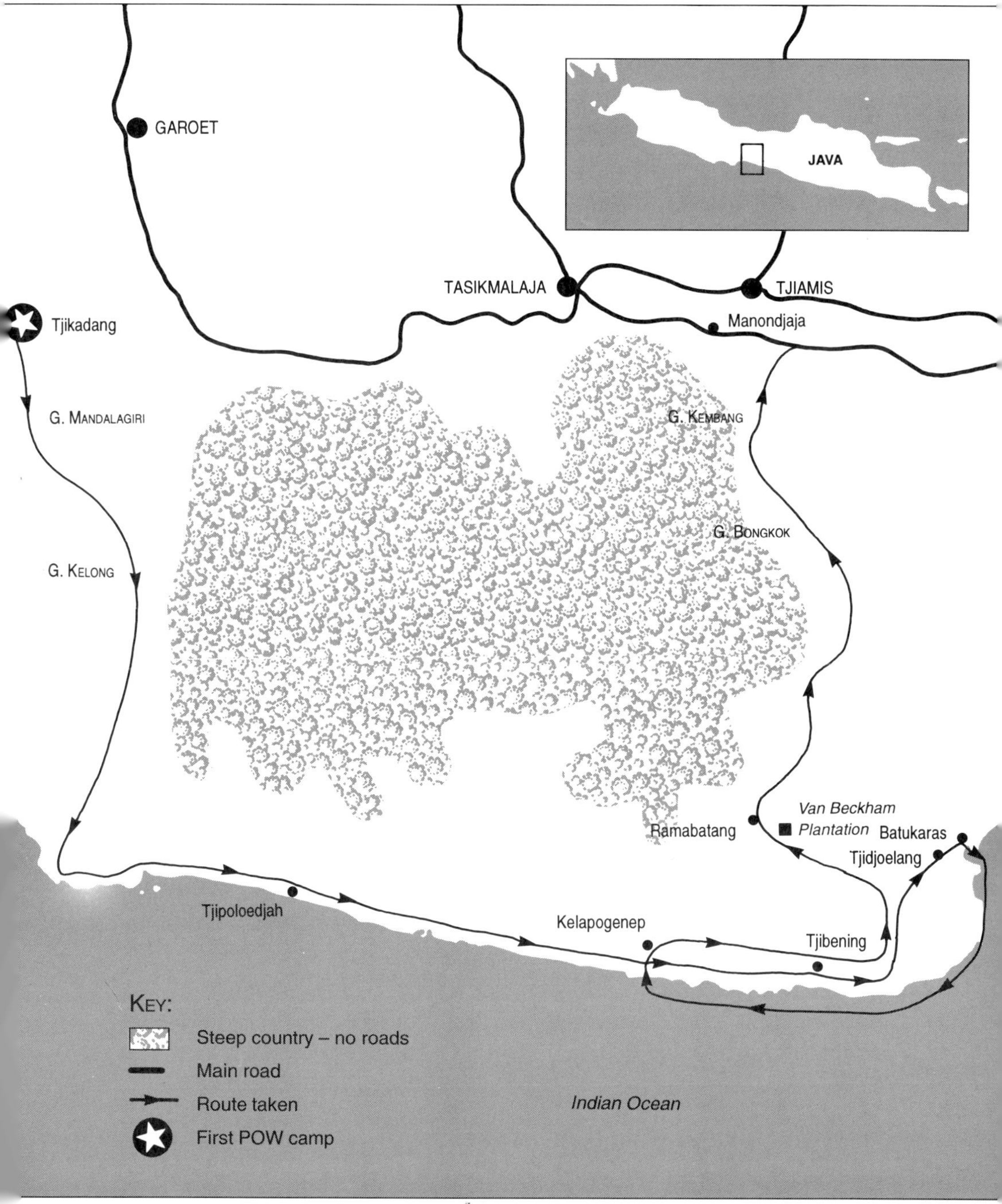

Away from it all — the route taken after escaping from the camp outside Tjikadiang.

village. Here we had a meal and the headman detailed a guide to show us our way to the next village. We felt fairly safe here as there were no roads, only tracks, and we were sure that no Japs would come on foot at this time. Even in these remote parts of Java there were numerous villages and we spent the next few nights in these.

Since our track petered out on the second day we trekked slowly over land through paddy fields, the irrigated fields of rice. They have to be flooded during most of the growing season for each crop. Each field is small and is bounded by an earth wall to lock in the water. Miles and miles of flat country are cultivated this way and the only paths are along the earth walls dividing the plots. These extend in terraces up quite steep hillsides in graceful patterns.

After the paddy fields we came to a narrow belt of jungle. Beyond it was the sea. Our guide had left us by now and we just took a compass course through the jungle. Until you are actually in this jungle you would imagine it to be heavy New Zealand bush, but once in it, what a difference: lovely palms that look exactly like the New Zealand native nikau, have long sharp thorns, and the undergrowth is difficult to force your way through.

Finally, just at evening, we broke through the last of the jungle and before us was the sea. My heart sank as I looked on a beautiful sandy beach. Instead of the smooth, calm waters of the north coast, great breakers from the ocean were crashing on the shore. This was no coast where you would find a boat hidden up a mangrove-covered creek, but a coast open to the full force of the Indian Ocean. I think I realised then that our chances of escape were very remote.

That night we slept on the sand draped in parachute silk, but were still were eaten by mosquitoes. In the morning the lovely white silk was spotted all over with blood. Quite early in the morning we started eastwards along the beach. Sometimes we had to detour inland to round some impassable rocks but for two days we kept close to the beach. Every native we met we asked "Kapal ada?" ("Is there a boat?"). Always the answer was "No," but that further eastwards there were plenty of boats. We spent our third night on the coast in a village called Tjipatoedjar, in company with four soldiers who had been sent to relieve Singapore. They were King's 3rd Hussars — Bradford, De Arden, Benson, and one whose name I cannot remember — and had been through the siege of Tobruk. It was a great evening. We had a wonderful meal of rice and bully beef and some eggs. These four had been living down the coast since the capitulation and had decided to give themselves up. When they heard that we meant to go on looking for a boat, two of them, De Arden and Benson, asked to come with us. I was happy about this as my Scots friend and I were not getting on very well together.

Since we had left camp the weather had been kind. On the nights we slept in the open it remained fine and all the days were the same. Now that we were in the wilds a day or so didn't seem to matter with me, but Eddie was in a real panic to get on and away, so the four of us set off again next morning.

From Tjipatoedjor the going was easier and for a great distance we followed a path often bordered by coconut palms. Sometimes we slept in a village, sometimes in a deserted atap hut*, and sometimes in the open.

The country through which we passed during this time was very interesting and beautiful. In our POW camp we had been in the high country amid tea. Tea country is most beautiful and when we came down towards the coast, though the scenery changed each day, it was still beautiful. Java has a background of high mountains, some of which, as in New Zealand, are volcanoes.

The natives were friendly and gave us rice and eggs as our rations had all been used up. For drink we usually had green coconuts. We couldn't climb the trees ourselves — De Arden tried, and made a horrible mess of his legs — but for a few cents the natives would scale nimbly up and throw down a few to us. Coconut water is delicious and a wonderful thirst quencher.

The two army men were good company. De Arden was a real fool and had us laughing half the time. Benson was a huge, quiet man, one you could depend on in any circumstances.

We saw hundreds of monkeys as we journeyed east. Snakes sometimes were lying asleep on the grassy path, and at times crocodiles went crashing through the long grass away from us. If we had only had more time and circumstances had been different we could have enjoyed it all. Each time we asked "Kapal ada?" we received the same reply. It was very discouraging as we were getting nearer and nearer to a part of the coast which we knew the Japs were occupying. At last we came to a village called Tjimerak. Here a Chinese shopkeeper gave us provisions. The

---

*Atap The basic roofing material of South East Asia is made by doubling long palm leaves around four-foot lengths of split bamboo, and lashing the leaves in sequence with thin strips of bamboo skin. This makes a sheet about four feet by two feet which is used to form roof and walls.

Chinese merchants held great sway in Java, controlled much of the country's business and were real friends to us.

We had now come, we knew, to the last stage of our quest. Only one other spot remained where we might possibly find a boat. Its name was Batoekeras and on my maps it was shown as a tiny inlet on the coast. We decided to try there, knowing that if we had no luck we would have to make up our minds: go back or give ourselves up. Batoekeras was a glorious little bay fringed with coconut palms, with white glistening sand and white breakers, ideal for surfing! The natives were kind — but there were no boats.

That evening the natives told us that the Japanese had repaired a bridge, had passed through the last village we had stayed in and captured some soldiers and taken them to Bandjar, a larger town where the enemy were established. It was bad news. It would not be safe to turn back. We decided on a long chance. Drawn up on the beach were two canoes, each was about 12 feet long, and built to carry about two or three people in calm water. We decided to buy both of them.

The natives charged us an exorbitant price for these two canoes, but with the help of one of them who was a bamboo craftsman, we joined the two together with thick, strong pieces of bamboo tied with lengths of bamboo skin: much better than nails. We fitted four cross-beams and made them look like miniatures of the old canoes that the first Maori are said to have used in their voyages to New Zealand.

We had no platform between the hulls. Our mast was bamboo, six or seven feet high. The sail was formed in the native fashion. Two pieces of light bamboo about 10 feet long were tied together at the bottom but spread about 7 feet apart at the top. In the V formed by these pieces my parachute silk was sewn around the bamboo. Since the glistening white silk would have been too obvious, we trampled it in the mud. It was surprising how long it took to make it dirty enough. We also had wooden paddles and so as not to lose them we tied them to the hulls. A larger paddle was our steering gear. It took us a day to do all this.

By sunset all was ready, so we invested in some chickens, had an enormous meal, and laid in food for our voyage. We were to try to sail our freak craft westwards along the coast and then cross the Sunda Strait to Sumatra, a distance of 60 or 70 miles. If we met any other craft we would try to signal for help and if possible seize the boat. We were armed, and desperate. If we managed to get to Sumatra we would try to get a larger craft and head for Ceylon. In Sumatra there were few invaders, and we thought we would be able to live for a long while on the west coast, searching for a vessel.

For water we took a great number of green coconuts and two four-gallon cans. Our food was rice and eggs plus some cooked chickens, and bananas. Not very much, but we felt that if necessary we could land somewhere on the coast and get more. We estimated that with good weather the trip would take three or four days.

Chapter 3

OUT TO SEA

Early in the morning we pushed our craft through the surf at the most sheltered part of the bay. We had a large audience to see us off. Most of the natives thought we were mad, but they were friendly, kind folk. Our craft was almost swamped in the surf, but we made it. We found after bailing out that we had only about 2 inches' freeboard. At first we paddled out to sea but when we were clear of the headland we hoisted our sail and started along the coast. All went well for a while. Up and down the long swells we rode, miraculously shipping no water. We estimated our speed at about four knots. For lunch we had some bananas, and two coconuts. Everything was going fine and our spirits began to rise.

About six hours after we had left the shore — perhaps about 2 p.m. — the clear sky clouded over and a strong breeze came up that rippled the surface of the swells. The wind increased, and the tops of the swells became white; soon we were shipping water at every wave, and it was only by continual bailing we could keep the canoes afloat.

Then it happened. We were all in the water, with the waves breaking over us. The canoes were upright, but below the surface of the water, only the mast showing. We tried to bail them out but it was useless, so we simply drifted with the wind. Fortunately the wind was blowing us towards the shore, and after a great deal of effort we managed to get the sail set again, and were steadily blown back to the land we had wanted to leave.

It was here that I was glad of Benson. He didn't panic as the other two did, but kept swimming hard with me to keep the bows pointed in the right direction. I enjoyed the first two or three hours in the water. I love swimming in the sea, and when we could enjoy a salvaged banana at the same time I thought it good fun.

Eventually we were close to land, but if we had kept our sail set we would have landed on some nasty rocks. We had to lower it and try to paddle our submarine craft towards a small beach. It took about an hour and a half to paddle this short distance, sitting in water up to our waists.

In trying to catch one big wave we got carried only a short way, and then we were left wallowing for another enormous one to break on top of us. Fortunately no one was hurt, and we were hurled on the beach. We had been in the water four and a half hours, so it was just sunset when we were tossed ashore. All our food was gone, and we had only the clothes in which we stood. I still had my Aussie hat. Luckily De Arden had some matches in a waterproof case, so we were able to light a fire. We shivered, we were hungry, but worst of all we were eaten by mosquitoes.

In the morning we found ourselves in a very desolate area. The beach was narrow, with only a little flat land behind it. High cliffs closed it in. Monkeys took a lively interest in us, and as we searched for a way up the cliffs, many small crocodiles crashed through the bushes. While the other three went in search of food, I stayed by the canoes until they came back. We had decided to have another try, and as well as food they were to try to get a native carpenter to help us rig the canoes again. We decided that if we took less food and water and one less crew we would have a better chance. De Arden was definitely not going to try again and was going to give himself up.

Later that day Ben came back and said that Eddie had decided on giving himself up and that they had talked him, Ben, into agreeing with them. It probably was the wisest thing for them to do, but I am afraid I lost my temper and abused them for their decision. I tore off the compass that hung around my neck and threw it into the wet sand. My small automatic I left in the fork of a tree, and I gave the maps to a native who gave Ben and me a meal as we tramped over the hills to rejoin the other two. Next morning the other three left for Bandjar to give themselves up. I rested until the next day and then started for the hills. I felt sure I could live there for the three months that would elapse before the Americans came.

The natives had told me that inland from Tjimerak was a plantation owned by a Dutchman called Van Beekam. I decided to call on him and see if he had any news. It was a long walk, and in the afternoon as I approached his bungalow it seemed as if no one was at home. Then, following the barking of his two huge Alsatian dogs, Van Beekam came to the door. I told him that I was on the run and had been down the coast, and asked if he could give me any news.

Van Beekam was one of the good Dutchmen I met. He asked me in for a cup of tea, and I met his lovely wife, who was also Dutch. They were very kind, and gave me a meal on their wide verandah. During this meal a native came with a message. The native was completely servile. He didn't come closer than about 40 or 50 yards until Van Beekam beckoned him, and then he came on his knees, gave the message and backed away. Van Beekam told me what was in the message The Japs had come into the district and might be paying him a visit. As soon as I heard this I wanted to leave, because of the terrible consequences to him if I was found there. He would have none of it, and made me stay the night. He said he would be warned if they were coming.

What a wonderful night it was. The Van Beekams washed my shorts and shirt and while these were drying I wore a pair of their pyjamas. I think that they were glad to have someone white to talk to. I was more than glad to talk and for a few short hours to be civilised again. And what a delight it was to sit down in pyjamas to a good meal with all the trimmings — fine glass, white napery, and shining cutlery!

During the evening I asked van Beekam's advice about trying to live in the hills. He said if he were in my shoes he would give it a go, but I must have some sort of weapon, maps and a compass. These he couldn't give me because the Japanese had confiscated all firearms. When I told him what I had left at the beach he urged me to try to recover them, even though it meant passing through Tjimerak again.

So, next morning, armed with a bundle of sandwiches, and dressed in clean clothes, I went back to the beach, about 15 miles away. In the afternoon my spirits were low again and I nearly gave up. The heat, the long march, and the terrible loneliness made me think that it wasn't worth the effort. I decided to leave it to fate. I would go to the beach, but if I couldn't find the gear I would give myself up. The gun I knew would be easy to find, and so would the maps. But the compass was only about the size of a wrist watch attached to a piece of string. I had flung it into the sand below high-water mark and it would be very hard to find.

I found the natives easily and retrieved the maps. The gun was still in the fork of the tree. But when I looked at the place where I thought I had thrown the compass it seemed impossible that it could ever be found. With a sharp stick I scratched systematically, hoping to catch the piece of string, but without any luck. I threw the stick away and gave up. But something made me go back to have just a few more scratches. On the second try I caught the string and pulled the compass out of the sand. I counted this an omen, and decided to go to the hills.

Chapter 4

HANDED OVER

It was completely dark when I got back to Tjimerak, and I went to the Chinese storekeeper for something to eat. I had a few guilders left and bought a sarong. He gave me some food and tea. While I ate my food the Chinese played Mah Jong for very large stakes. I was afraid to stay in Tjimerak as the Japs could arrive here by car, so I set off in the dark for the plantation.

At last I could trudge no further, and seeing a light approaching I stopped a native and asked him for a place to sleep. He was very afraid of me, but took me to a building nearby. I was so tired that I had only one thought and that was to sleep, so I didn't notice much about the building. Inside, two young men lounged in one corner and at the other end an old man was on his knees praying. I gave the boys a cigarette each. The old man stopped praying and came and took one too, and then returned to his prayers. I said "Tidor" (Sleep) — one of the few words of Malay I then knew, and pointed to a corner. They both nodded, and in a few minutes I was asleep.

How long I slept I have no idea, but I was awakened by someone shaking me violently. As I came to I became aware of a crowd of natives, some of them shouting, and quickly realised I must leave. I had been trying to sleep in the House of Islam, which I gathered would not be countenanced, so once again I set off into the dark night. Fortunately the moon came out quite soon, and I was able to travel fairly comfortably.

It was too early to wake the Van Beekams when I reached the plantation, so I slept for about an hour before I went up to the house. Once again they welcomed me and I had a meal and set off again on my own. Van Beekam had told me I could stay in an empty bungalow on the far edge of his plantation, so I made for this as it was on my route to the hills. All along the track natives greeted me with "Tabi Tuan" — (Good day Master) — and I was given fruit and a coconut to drink. At the bungalow I handed a note to the headman, and he unlocked the house for me. I had walked almost continuously for 30 hours, so again my one concern was sleep. I lay on the floor in one of the rooms and was almost asleep when some noise made me look up at the window. It was crowded with faces having a look at the strange white man. But sleep was still what I wanted most, and regardless of the publicity I was soon off.

I was awakened by footsteps coming into the house. I'm afraid I swore, but it was the headman with a coconut for me to drink. He left me, and I was almost asleep again when more footsteps came. Two pairs this time. I cursed silently, wondering would I ever get to sleep. It was kindness herself in the persons of the headman and his wife. They brought me a complete meal. Then at last I was left to sleep.

Next day I did a short march and arrived at Tjigoergoer. There the headman was very kind and I was given a room in the meeting house. The room was very clean and the floor was covered with grass mats. There was also a bed, covered with a grass mat. The headman came over later and sat while I was served with a most wonderful meal of rice, bamboo shoots, spiced meat, fish, fried bananas and a wonderfully hot curry. When I went to bed one of the natives brought two pots of tea to last me through the night.

I was told that at a place not far away and on the track to the hills was another Dutch plantation. This sounded good to me, and I thought I would be able to find some news. Langkaptantjar, where the owner of the plantation lived, was miles from any road. The only way to it was on foot or horseback, yet when I met this Dutchman he turned pale and wouldn't even speak to me. He was so frightened of doing anything the distant Japs would find out about.

The native headman, though — a man who did not even share with me the bond of colour — was very kind and gave me a great meal. He also insisted on giving me a blanket, which I used constantly. This generous person also insisted on guiding me to the next village. The track was very wild. We descended into a river bed and waded across the river, then climbed again up a very winding path, to arrive at Tjisoroea in the dark. My guide had a talk with the headman of this village, and I was installed once again in the local meeting-house. I was very surprised when my good friend the guide said goodbye and started home in the darkness. I hadn't dreamt that he wouldn't stay the night in the village.

I was not very impressed with my new host so I left early in the morning. I didn't know it, but by then I must have been sickening for malaria, and I found the going very hard indeed. Also, I was nearly covered with some tropical skin disease which was spreading all over my body. Van

Beekam had given me a bottle of Dettol and whenever I came to a suitable stream I bathed these horrible-smelling sores. They were full of a yellow watery pus, and as I was covered beneath my shirt and shorts my clothes would stick to me and were hard to take off. The next night I slept in one of the tiny atap shelters that had been built to give shade to the bird-frighteners in a dry paddy field. With my sarong and the blanket I kept fairly free from mosquito bites. In the morning I was met by the local native policeman. He was riding a grey horse. He led me to his house and gave me a breakfast of rice and fried banana. His wife was very beautiful and not as dark as the usual natives, but when she smiled I was shocked to see that her teeth were quite black through chewing betel nut. My host allowed me to use their combined shower and lavatory. This was built over a pool containing fish. Water was carried into this hut and poured continuously through the slatted bamboo floor from a bamboo pipe about 2 feet above the floor. To have a shower you just knelt beneath the pipe. When you used the lavatory, which was a hole in the floor, there was a great rush of fish. Crude sanitary arrangements, but with a lot to be said in their favour; a food-producer, too, because the owner eats the fish.

The road I took when I left these hospitable people was still climbing, and before evening cloud came down, and as I could hardly see the track I stopped at the first house I came to — only a few miles on the way. It was large, and I asked for food and a place to sleep. When I was shown inside I wondered at the number of raised bamboo platforms all around the walls, but after a good meal of rice I was soon asleep. I was awakened during the night. All around me were sleeping bodies — I suppose about 50 of them. My shelter for the night was the lodging house for the native porters who carried sugar up from the coastal strip to Tasikmalaya. The cost, at this place, for dinner, bed and breakfast was five cents — about twopence in our currency of the day.

The next day I marched wearily on towards Manondjaja, a town about eight miles away on one of the main roads of Java. If I could cross this road I would then be in a mountainous region like the country I had just passed through, but with even fewer tracks. I decided to try to get to the road, and cross it that night. But something was wrong with me. My head seemed to be on fire, and my body ached in every part. By now I was almost entirely covered with these horrible sores, and I stank to high heaven. I stopped once or twice to bathe the sores, and could hardly get enough energy to start off again. The natives were kind — one gave me two eggs, which I sucked raw, and another gave me a bunch of bananas. At these little expressions of sympathy my eyes watered and I nearly cried. At about three in the afternoon I came to a village called, I think, Tjimeum, and I just tumbled into the corner of a room in a shop.

I don't remember anything about this time except that I took some quinine — a huge dose of about twelve tablets — that Van Beekam had given me. In the morning of, I think, the next day I was clear-headed but terribly weak and sick. I decided I must give myself up and get treatment or I would die. From Tjimeum to Manondjaja is only about three miles. It took me all day to reach Manondjaja. I have no recollection of the trip except walking down the tarsealed road in Manondjaja, just at sunset, stared at by hundreds of native faces. I was then barefoot, bearded, and dressed in an old pair of shorts and a torn shirt. I have never felt so completely alone.

A well-dressed native came out from a building and addressed me in English. What a pleasant surprise! He told me he was the assistant wedana (assistant magistrate) and asked if he could do anything to help. I said I was sick and wanted to give myself up to the Japanese, as I couldn't carry on any further. He took me to a very kindly old man who was the wedana for the district. I was given food and a bath, and more food. The wedana also called one of his native policemen and spoke to him as I was drinking a cup of coffee. The policeman pedalled off on his bicycle and when he returned about half an hour later he handed me a pair of army boots, a battle dress, tunic, and some shorts. Evidently he knew natives who had these articles as loot. The wedana gave me bandages, medicine and some packets of cigarettes.

Best news of all, the wedana, who was pro-British, arranged with the Japs by telephone to take me to the British POW camp at Tasikmalaya — the place from which the final desperate flight of our two last Vildebeestes had been made about six weeks before. He drove me to Tasikmalaya in his own car, and as we passed through the camp gates I had a fleeting glimpse of my first Japanese guard. I was duly handed over to the camp CO, who gave the wedana a receipt. The wedana left after giving me a great bunch of bananas.

One of the officers gave up his bed to me and a doctor came and examined me. I was soon asleep. I believe I was delirious for some time, but back amongst my own people, I soon recovered.

Chapter 5

TASIKMALAYA CAMP

Tasikmalaya camp was on one corner of the aerodrome from which we had operated before the capitulation. The officers were housed in one hangar and the airmen in another. The sergeants and Warrant Officers were in a small shed between the two.

We had been led to understand that the camp would be a permanent one, so all the energetic men were busily making themselves comfortable. Beds had been made from old pieces of timber and sacks, from bamboo and from wire. Some of the officers still had their camp beds and there were a lot of good, thick, kapok mattresses out in the sun each morning. Everyone had mosquito netting.

The food was very good and was still the normal army rations. Just out of camp was a native market and there we could purchase, if we had any money, eggs, all manner of fruits, cigarettes, condensed milk and bread. An Australian officer, Lieutenant Patty, was in charge of quite a large sum of money donated by the Australian people for the comfort of the troops overseas. Patty treated me as an Aussie and gave me small sums of money periodically. It was greatly appreciated, and allowed me to buy extra food.

We were allowed out of camp in the afternoon and had to be back quite early. Each time we passed the guard house we had to salute if we were wearing hats and bow if not. Working parties were organised by the camp guard and each morning and afternoon these parties repaired the aerodrome or worked at loading and unloading trains. In Tasikmalaya the work was not very hard and the guards seemed almost in awe of the British boys at times. There were a few incidents but nothing very serious — at least not by comparison with what was to become commonplace later, though even in this comparatively placid atmosphere the guards let drop an occasional hint of their ideas about corrective treatment for erring POWs.

If anyone had struck a Japanese or tried to escape or even failed to bow to the guards he would be beaten up in front of the full parade of

POWs. One or two guards would beat the culprit with their fists until they knocked him down, and then would kick him until he was insensible. These callous beatings were horrible to watch. I suppose they served their purpose, for after witnessing punishment such as this you would think twice about "trying anything on".

The British Commanding Officer of this camp was a very fine type indeed, Wing Commander Stedman. We were also fortunate in having two very good doctors and a first-class hospital was organised in a shed. At this time there was a good supply of medicine and surgical gear. Not many men were sick, only a few who had malaria and a few with dysentery. Most of the patients were out-patients whose complaints were chiefly tropical ulcers and sores. The camp had also three padres so that the spiritual needs of the men should not have been neglected.

For two or three days I was very ill and unable to realise my good fortune in falling into such a happy camp. I had dreaded an interrogation by the Japanese, for if they had found out that I had escaped from another camp they would have shot me. That was the rule. However, after my illness alone in the hills I felt wonderfully secure and I had my kindly old wedana of Manondjaja to thank for it all. The officer who had given up his comfortable bed to me slept on the floor. He was Flight Lieutenant Mason, commonly called Tiny because of his huge size. He was a grand chap and a great friend to me afterwards.

When I was sufficiently clear-headed to take note of things I found that I was almost completely wrapped in bandages. Fortunately the sores healed quickly with the proper treatment, and in a few days I was living with the other sergeants and the WOs. They were a good crowd of chaps. Though I was practically penniless they never failed to include me in sharing the extra food they bought. One of our greatest treats was to poach a couple of eggs and have them on toast. There was a forge in the hangar and it was going almost continuously.

This was one of the very happy times of my captivity, for each day I was feeling better and could do a little more. But on my tenth day in the camp, malaria hit me again and I was sent into the camp hospital. For three weeks I stayed there, receiving wonderful treatment. During this period I had a visit from Brad — one of the army chaps whom we had met down the coast. Brad and I became good friends, and we stayed together for about two years after this. After we had parted down the coast these boys had just made their way slowly back to give themselves up, living with the natives as I had done.

Corporal Bradford was stockily built and had a happy, round face usually covered with very black whiskers. When he grinned, which was often, there was a gaping hole where two teeth were missing, and this gave him a very wild look. Some of the boys recoiled from it, but this only amused him more. In everyday life Brad's humour would have been deplored, but in this life things were different, and I thought him pure gold.

The padres, in my experience, were a different story. My impression of the three in our camp was that they were too preoccupied with the welfare of their own bodies to spend much time on the souls of the men. It was a wonderful opportunity for them to show their religion to the men, but I never saw any sign of it. I thought that one of the first duties of a padre was to visit the sick, yet although I was in hospital for three weeks in this camp I know of not one visit by a padre to the hospital. I am sorry to say it, but this was to be typical of my experience of padres all through my years of imprisonment. There was one exception: Father P.J. Rorke,* a Roman Catholic padre who continuously worked for the welfare of the prisoners; but I met him later.

When I came out of hospital I wasn't made to work, so I busied myself constructing a comfortable bed, and making a few items. I was very proud of the knives I made. On the aerodrome were some wrecked ack-ack guns. From these I managed to get some pieces of stainless steel from which I fashioned, on the forge and anvil, two very useful knives. One of them was heavy, and good for chopping down pieces of wood into wooden shoes which we called "clompers". This knife was successfully smuggled into three camps and must have been used to make hundreds of "clompers". The other knife was a vicious-looking "pig-sticker" type and I ditched it after one other camp because it was not so useful, and the Japanese would have given me a terrible bashing if they found it.

During this time we saw few Japanese, just the guards and an occasional officer who came and saw our CO. But one day a carload arrived. They were talking with the CO for a long time, and when they left he

*Father Patrick Rorke SJ, who came from Kingston-upon-Thames, Surrey, died at Birmingham on 2 September 1990, in the care of Sisters of the Poor. He was 86. An obituary by John F.X. Harriott in the *Tablet* for that month described him as "a man, a priest, a Jesuit, with an absolute passion for God", and quoted a Surrey barber who had known him as a POW. He was a "solid gold hero" who voluntarily took beatings and other indignities in place of men too weak to endure them. He also sold pages from his breviary to guards who smoked, in order to buy food that others needed.

went with them. I never heard of him again. The Japanese wanted him to give permission for the officers to fill in a questionnaire, and he refused. As they were taking him away someone asked about his baggage and the Japanese replied that where the CO was going he wouldn't want any gear. I don't know what happened to him, but rumour had it that he was tortured and killed. Wing Commander Vines, who took over afterwards, gave the permission they demanded and there was no further trouble.

Almost immediately we were told that we had to move camp. This was a great disappointment. We were allowed to take only as much gear as we could carry, so it was difficult to sort out what to discard and what to keep. We were each issued with a fair share of the camp store of food, mostly bully beef. Some of us had great meals of it before leaving, rather than discard some other article.

Just at daybreak we were paraded, and after being counted were given the order to march. It was quite a few miles to the station and I, still weak from my spell in hospital, had great difficulty in keeping going, but eventually we arrived and were crowded into train carriages. These were the kind used for the natives and were very rough and uncomfortable. I have very little recollection of the trip. All we knew was that we were travelling eastwards with frequent stops, but we weren't allowed off the train.

While the train was in motion we were allowed to have the windows open, but during the long waits at some small stations we nearly suffocated in the heat. My malaria, which was to accompany me wherever I went, attacked me again, and I had a very miserable time.

Eventually, I think after a day and a night in the train, we arrived at Surabaya, and were marched to a school. It was labelled Lyceum so we always called this place Lyceum Camp. During the search of our belongings just after we arrived the Japs discovered one of my knives and threw it into a pile of other things they had confiscated. Fortunately, one of the chaps retrieved it when the Japs weren't looking. I was very ill by the time the search was over and was taken to the camp hospital.

Chapter 6

LYCEUM CAMP

Rooms in Lyceum Camp were built round a number of squares of lawn and there were passages connecting all of them together. High stone walls surrounded the complete school, so that it was already rather like a jail. At one end there was a playing field, which was used for parades and also for soccer and rugby. A massive gateway with rooms on either side was taken over by the Japanese as their guardroom. When we arrived, the school was already occupied by Dutch and British prisoners, and our arrival caused serious overcrowding. In fine weather the former squares of lawn were squares of hard-packed mud, but in the wet — and we spent a rainy season in this camp — they were quagmires. Most of the prisoners slept on the tiles. Some had camp stretchers or mattresses — the majority had to endure the hard, cold tiles with only a grass mat to soften them.

A senior Dutch officer ran the camp, but was helped by the British officers. The food we thought shocking. Later we were going to think back with longing to the food in this camp, but just after Tasikmalaya, where we had had ordinary army rations, it seemed to us very poor stuff. Breakfast was a measure of watery boiled rice which we called "pap". It was almost all water, and passed through us in a very short time. Lunch was a small loaf of bread about the size of a bun. The most enjoyable way to eat these buns was to toast them and spread over them a little coconut or peanut oil — when we were able to buy any. Our evening meal was the best of the day and consisted of rice cooked beautifully dry, and some stew. Fortunately we had some Dutch cooks who knew how to prepare the strange vegetables we were now fed on. Most of these stews were flavoured with spices and all had chillies in them.

A small working party was required by the Japanese each day and it was considered lucky to be included in the party as they allowed the prisoners to buy food and cigarettes in the rest periods. For each day's toil a private received ten cents as his wages, and a sergeant or W.O. fifteen cents. At this time food was cheap and with these wages quite a lot of extra food could be bought. Fruit was especially cheap, and just what was needed to make our diet sufficient. The gulf between conditions for the officers and the men was very wide, in this and all other camps. Officers received a fixed sum each month and were not compelled to work. Some of them, however, always went with the working parties here and took charge of them.

The internal duties of the camp were organised by the senior officers, and the Japanese carried out inspections periodically to see that the camp was kept clean and tidy. Each night we all, excepting the sick and those on duty, had a parade for "tenko". We were counted and recounted, then the room commanders had to give the number of sick in quarters, and if the total was correct we could break off parade. If, however, there was a discrepancy in the figures, we all stayed on parade until the mistake or the body was found. Often we were on parade for hours. Each time we saw a guard we were required to stand to attention and either bow or salute. The first person to see a guard approach was duty bound to spring to attention and shout "Kyotsky, Kiri",(attention, bow or salute) and when all had done this we were told to "Yesame!" (rest).

To fail to do this was one of the greatest crimes, and usually meant a severe beating for the person the guard thought should have shouted the commands. Sometimes it meant that the whole room was punished by being made to stand to attention for hours.

Another serious crime was, of course, to try to escape. This didn't happen very often because if caught (and the chances of getting away must have been about a million to one) the escapers were shot or tortured. No person escaped from any camp that I was in, except two Ambonese. They were soon caught and were made what the Japanese considered a suitable example. They were tied by their necks to two palm trees near the guardroom, so that they could only move in a small circle, and for weeks were tortured quietly for amusement by the guards. They must have been given food, for they survived for a long time and then disappeared. They were kicked and beaten about all day, and I suppose all night. The guards used to stump out cigarettes on their bare skin. I heard later that one died and the other went mad. Some prisoners in a camp outside Surabaya were shot because they sneaked out to the village to buy some food.

In camp we learned to queue for everything — for showers, for food, and no less for the latrines, which were so overcrowded that some open ones had to be dug in the corner of our parade ground. It became a serious crime to break in on a queue. The poor food and crowded conditions gradually brought disease. There was a great deal of dysentery; not the diarrhoea that you know at home, but bacillary dysentery, a foul disease that seems to tie your stomach in tight knots while you pass blood and slime almost continuously. Fortunately, we had medicine to cure this disease fairly quickly, but it left us weak and exhausted, ready victims for diseases of malnutrition such as beriberi and pellagra.

Scurvy, caused by lack of vitamin C, became a common complaint. We found our lips and mouths becoming ulcerated and sore. Each morning on waking our lips were stuck together at the corners of our mouths. We also went about continuously scratching our scrotums; we were in agony from them.

One small orange per man would probably have keep the camp free of this vitamin C deficiency. Our senior medical officer pleaded with the Japanese to send in fruit, but the little they sent was not sufficient. Fruit at this time was very cheap. Oranges were only about half a cent each, bananas about one cent. In this camp we had twelve or thirteen officers with the rank of Wing Commander or Lieutenant Colonel, and while they were always wanting to buy cigarettes at 20 guilders a carton, they made no attempt to alleviate the sickness of the men by buying fruit out of their allowances. Twenty guilders would have bought two oranges for every man in the camp.

In this camp we had a cheery bunch of sailors. Their discipline and general cleanliness were an example to the rest of the camp. They were sailors from the destroyer *Jupiter* which was sunk in the Sunda Strait in an epic battle about which I learnt more later. Their commander was Commander Thew — known as "Fix It". He was wounded in the leg but he was always pushing for better food and conditions for the men. Often he was so insistent to the Japanese that he was beaten up, but he earned their respect by his perseverance and courage.

In this camp I was the only New Zealander for most of the time. We all had to wear a number; it was a great crime to be seen without your number. On this small card was also printed, in Japanese, one's nationality. Often the guards used to stop me and ask in Malay where New Zealand was. My stock reply was Australia, and they seemed satisfied; they had heard of Australia.

After I moved out of hospital I was allotted a corner of a room next to my friend Brad. I made a rough bed out of some planks I had found, and it kept me off the cold floor. It was a very happy nook, this corner of ours.

We arranged shelves on the wall and in a very primitive way made ourselves comfortable. We decided that we would each give a bit of a talk about something interesting and two or three times a week one of us would hold forth. These talks were most enlightening and became a regular feature of our small corner.

We organised other people in the camp to come and lecture to us, too. In these sessions we had a most interesting series on psychic science, and one on the motion picture industry. We had talks about Australia, Canada, America and England. I gave one or two on New Zealand. I found most people very interested in my own small country.

During this period we had a serious brush with authority in the form of a crowd of WOs and sergeants who, after casting envious eyes at the comfortable corner we had created for ourselves, tried to oust us. Higher aid was sought, but even the threat of a court-martial after the war couldn't move us as we were sure of our rights. Most of this time I was either having malaria or recovering from it, and was unable to go on a working party.

The days slowly passed with the same monotonous routine, and for the first time in my life I had nothing to do but think. I am sure malaria (or perhaps the quinine you take) makes your mind very active. I was able to read quite a number of good books, including Wells' *Outline of History*. One of the officers in the camp lectured us on the universe, and again on evolution. One man had a first edition of James Joyce's *Ulysses* and a copy of James Branch Cabell's novel, *Jurgen*. I myself had copies of Eric Linklater's *Juan in America*, and *Juan in China*, and I was able to exchange these for many others.

In the dry spells I spent most of the time between meals and parades lying in the hot sun. We found that although the sun was scorchingly hot we were not seriously troubled by sunburn. Dutchmen told us that pneumonia was the worst illness of the Dutch army, and I am sure our medical men were worried about it, but it was practically unheard of. In my opinion this was simply because we wore hardly any clothes, and let the sun on to our bodies. I didn't realise it at the time, but this was the happiest period of my captivity.

Chapter 7

LYCEUM TO DARMO

After we had been in Lyceum Camp about three or four months a very strange thing happened to the prisoners in Surabaya district. I don't think it happened anywhere else. It started, as all news did, with rumours. Someone had heard from someone else, and it was pukka gen, that the Japanese were going to allow relatives and friends of the POWs into the camp. The first inkling that it was true was when the Dutch were told to send in the names of their next of kin. The day or so following the guards told our officers that August 8 (I think that was the right date) was the day in which visitors would be allowed into the camp.

The Japanese must have been very sure of themselves at this time, or perhaps one of the local commanders was off celebrating a Nippon victory — I have no idea. But it was a great day. The gates were opened after lunch and immediately a great crowd of Dutch rushed in, frantically looking for their men. All were laden with goods, and some had brought servants to carry the huge parcels as well. We British troops were naturally left right out of it, and felt rather homesick and lonely. Some of the Dutch brought parcels for the British boys, but it was essentially a Dutch show.

While walking about with a friend of mine who had been in Singapore for a long time before the war I was suddenly surprised to see him embraced by a very well-dressed lady who showered him with kisses. This lady, a Belgian woman, had known Hector in Singapore and had come into the camp hoping to see some British people from that part. She was a very brave woman, for when she learned that we needed sulpha tablets she volunteered to come each Wednesday night just after dark and throw some over the wall. We told her that it was too dangerous a game and that if she were caught she would be beaten up. She assured us she knew what would happen but that she would be there on Wednesday night. Meeting her was one of the highlights of that day.

Each Wednesday night a parcel of sulpha tablets was thrown over. Sometimes I went with Hector to wait and receive it. It was a dangerous game for us, but doubly so for her. Once we were nearly caught, and but for the stupidity of the Japanese we would have been half killed. Then, after a few weeks, parcels ceased to arrive and we wondered what had happened to our friend. We never learned.

At last our afternoon was over, and helped along by guards who didn't mind using their rifle butts, the last visitors were ushered out of the camp. There was one amusing incident. One of our men got carried out with the rush of visitors and had almost to plead to be allowed to come in again. For about two days we ate enormously, for a great deal of the food brought was perishable, and the Dutch sent it to the cookhouse to be distributed through the camp. Also, they didn't want their usual rations and so we benefited doubly. For months afterwards the Dutch prisoners had tins of food to open for special occasions.

Our eating spree was soon over, and we settled down again to our dull routine. Not long after this the guards' tempers seemed to get worse and we had to be most careful. They built a bamboo cage in the parade ground and people who had displeased them were locked inside it during the day, and at night tied up beside the guard house. Often we were paraded to watch punishment of some unfortunate POW, and it was a horrible experience.

Some weeks after this I was found by the orderly sergeant and told to dress hurriedly in my best — which meant putting on my shirt — and report to the guards immediately. I wondered why, as no one else had to go with me from our courtyard, and my heart sank. To go to the Japs usually meant trouble. Followed by friendly cries of "Good luck Tommy!" I made my way to the office.

For quite a long time I had to stand to attention with about six other men. I realised when I saw my companions that the interview had to do with flying, as seven of us were pilots. There were two Amercians, one Canadian and three English. After some time we were divided, and sent into two rooms. I was with the two Americans. A Japanese captain then gave us a series of tests. One was to assemble a jigsaw puzzle while he kept the time with a stopwatch. We had to add long columns of figures, again with the captain timing us. Another test was to assemble in the right sequence about 30 cylinders of exactly the same size but with the slightest difference in weight. There were other tests which I have forgotten.

It was 8 a.m. when we started, and about 4 p.m. when we finished, and then we were ordered to leave the room. We found all our possessions packed and waiting for us, and we were marched out of the camp.

Not only we ourselves but the whole camp wondered what was in store for us.

We hadn't long to wait, for after a short march we came to another POW camp — Jaarmarkt camp — and were given a place to sleep. We were able to mix with the others and had a great time trying to find old friends or learning news of them. Here we found the food better, but most of the buildings looked rather dilapidated. We also learned that a party of pilots had left this camp in the afternoon, and we surmised that they would probably be undergoing the same tests as those we had been through. Later we learned that we had been sent to Jaarmarkt so that we couldn't possibly talk to any of these pilots before they went through the tests. It was a very pleasant interlude, and we were disappointed that we were marched back to Lyceum next day. Why the Japanese conducted these tests I have no idea, unless it was to try to compare the mental efficiency of our pilots with theirs.

We returned to the old routine. There was a rumour that we were going to move. We heard rumours all the time about all sorts of things, and we came to believe that if a rumour persisted long enough there was something in it. This rumour of a move kept coming up for a number of weeks, and then suddenly we were ordered to be ready to leave camp. No one knew of our destination but there were many surmises. Some said Japan, some said Singapore. On the evening before we left we were told we would have a walk of about eight miles, but we still didn't know where we were going. The camp moved out early in the morning and, with frequent stops, we marched until we came to an old Dutch army barracks called Darmo.

Darmo was in the open fields and, though surrounded with wire and patrolled by guards, we could see out over the green landscape to the hills. It was a healthy camp. We had to work in the gardens but the hours were not long, and the food was better than Lyceum. Airy huts roofed with tiles and with the sides made of bamboo were allotted to us, and we slept not on the ground, but on a wide bench of bamboo that ran the length of the hut on each side. Each hut housed about a hundred men. The benches were about 6 feet 6 inches wide, and each man was allowed 3 feet of this, so that he had an area of 6 feet 6 inches by 3 feet. On this he slept, ate his meals and, in fact, did practically everything. These arrangements were far superior to those at Lyceum. The sanitary conditions were better, too.

Sport was encouraged and soccer was played every afternoon. Even in this camp, however, many were still suffering from vitamin C deficiency. Yet before I left Darmo my scurvy had disappeared, and strangely enough, though many times later conditions of living were far, far worse than any we had had up until then, I did not again have any effects from vitamin C deficiency. A man's body must be able somehow to adapt itself to C deficiency. Unfortunately this was not so with some of the other vitamins.

I mentioned earlier the gulf between the officers and the men which was apparent in each camp. I visited an officer friend in the camp hospital at Darmo. He was having bacon and eggs for his meal, and a private next to him was eating pap. Money talks everywhere, and money in a prison camp shouted.

I have very few recollections of Darmo, chiefly because it was a good camp. I don't remember many bashings. There were some, but not many. As I write this I have been wondering where I spent Christmas of 1942. It must have been a colourless day, or I am sure I would remember some incident of it. Of one thing I am certain: it was about the end of December that we were once again ordered to move. This time our move was tinged with regret. Darmo had been a good camp; perhaps the next one could be good too.

Chapter 8

JAARMARKT CAMP

Jaarmarkt camp had been a fairground. On most fairgrounds there is a motley collection of buildings, but seldom so motley as on a fairground used by Dutch, Javanese and Chinese. The main exhibition hall was a very large, well constructed building, but around it were scattered weird and wonderful structures. The Chinese houses were adorned with great red and gold dragons and were in the oddest of shapes. They were set about completely at random and to move around at night was a real Chinese puzzle; it was just as well we were enforced teetotallers.

In this camp there were approximately 5000 men, mostly Dutch and English, with a few Indians and Chinese. The POWs were housed in the existing buildings and in some long atap huts built specially for them. I was glad to be housed in one of the atap huts as they were cooler, and if a roof leaked it was easily repaired.

Discipline in Jaarmarkt was very rigid. A huge Korean whom we called "The Bull" was responsible for this. He was greatly feared by us, and also by the guards, most of whom were Koreans too. In this camp any man who saw a Jap guard approaching and failed to give a stentorian yell of "Kyotsky, Kiri,Yesame!" was in really bad trouble. Usually it was collective punishment and a whole hut would have no evening meal, or would have to stand to attention for several hours while the guards watched intently for movements of relaxation so that the unfortunate one would be beaten up for amusement.

Each morning at sunrise we were paraded for tenko. Tenko was always a worrying time. Any hut commander who hadn't got his figures right was in for a bashing. We had to number in Japanese and all orders were given in Japanese, in an attempt to build up Jap prestige. It was very difficult to remember the Japanese words and shout one's number correctly in the tense atmosphere of one of these parades.

Of course, working parties were carefully counted, and we spent hours standing about until the tenko was correct. The evening tenko was especially trying, as the Bull and his henchman tried to catch us out in every way. Usually more than 500 men were lined up in four ranks. There was always a struggle to be in the rear ones which did not count. Often the front rank, in trying to number, broke down. It seemed to delight the guards to be able to bash up the miserable POW responsible, and the count would start again.

"Bango!" (number) our officer would shout, and we would wait breathlessly, hoping no one would slip up in his counting, but it was an easy thing to do, for we had to count sometimes up to and over 200 in Japanese. Sometimes the Japs very craftily dismissed the front rank if they had numbered correctly and then made the other ranks do it again and again until they, too, counted correctly. This waiting about after a long hard day's work in the tropical sun completely exhausted us.

After the early morning parade we were ordered to face the rising sun and, led by the Bull, we were supposed to pray to the Nipponese gods. I don't imagine the gods liked our efforts much because there was some shocking abuse hurled at them and the Japs and their ancestors. After a time the Japanese suspected that the murmur of voices was not always dutiful when following the Bull in his incantations, and a watch was set. Quite a few who had been foolish enough to let their facial expressions betray them were given a cruel beating, and our hut commanders were severely warned.

More working parties were now being required by the Japanese each day, and the tempo of the work had increased. Our work outside was of all kinds. Sometimes we were stacking full drums of petrol about 6 feet high, sometimes cleaning and stacking empties. Sometimes we were on spade and shovel work digging air raid trenches and gun emplacements, at other times it was dock work, but the worst work of all was shifting bombs. The bombs were in clumsy cases, difficult to handle and terribly heavy after we had been carrying them for a few hours. A guard who caught anyone not working hard would strike him with anything handy — a piece of bamboo, or a rifle butt. Working party guards were almost always Japanese, the camp guards Koreans. We hated them even more.

There was one bright spot in the dreariness of Jaarmarkt. Depending on the place of work and the guard, food could still be bought outside, but the prices had risen. Any food or cigarettes so bought had to be smuggled into the camp, and it meant a beating and confiscation of the goods if you were caught. Here I learned to admire the Dutch women for their courage. In spite of repeated threats, beatings and sometimes shots, some of these women would find out where we were working and in some way

Saving Face — By Order Colonel Anami was a Japanese prison-camp commander in Java, whose beard earned him the nicknames of "Nitty Whiskers" and "Orang Kambing" (goat-man). The beard was composed of but a few hairs dangling from his chin, but, despite its oriental sparseness, Anami was rather proud of it. When he noticed the luxuriant European growths of the prisoners, representing the cultivation of a year or so, he issued the order in the last picture. This drawing was made by Flt.-Lieut. S.E. Scales, of New Zealand, who was a prisoner-of-war in Java.

get to us gifts of chocolate and cigarettes.

At first we felt very self-conscious about being marched through the streets of Surabaya, but after a while we became used to it and, tired as we usually were, even tried to march well. At times we were driven to work in trucks and this was a terrifying experience, for we were crowded on to the trays of these trucks which had no sides to hold us in. We kept ourselves from falling off by clinging to one another so that we were a solid mass of humanity which swayed into the turns of the road.

At Jaarmarkt an artist called Shepherd did a drawing of me; with my long beard and my Aussie hat I looked like a tough old Aussie of about fifty. Without the hat I looked even worse, for we all had to have shaven heads. If our hair grew more than a quarter of an inch long we were punished. However, even this head shaving had its bright side for a few. The Japs paid any barbers amongst the POWs to keep the hair of the men cut. It was a good job and barbers were a privileged class. One of them, Sergeant Brown (an Aussie) was our barber and he made a beautiful job of my ginger beard. Other privileged people in the camps were watchmakers and carpenters, as at times they had to work for the Japanese and were generously rewarded with food and cigarettes.

The Japanese usually gave us a certain amount of work to do each day but we always found that if, by special effort, we did it quickly so that we could return to camp early, they merely increased the amount of work to be done. We therefore worked as slowly as we dared, always watching the guards so that they wouldn't catch us loafing. As the guard looked our way we did a few strokes, but as soon as his back was turned we stopped. I soon decided that the only way to exist on these working parties was to avoid hard work as much as possible, and by continuous vigilance I did the minimum. After a time it became a sixth sense, this constant awareness of what the guards were doing.

Chapter 9

CULINARY

We got to know the guards well and what sort of treatment we could expect from them, and we gave them names. There was Black Face, Tiger, Stupid and Pig Face. Not all of them I am sure were really cruel, but the kinder ones were afraid to be nice. Occasionally, if no other Japanese were in sight, one of these kinder guards would tell us to rest and would sometimes even buy some fruit and give us cigarettes. Even the most callous of them seemed very homesick. At times during the rest periods they would talk to us in Malay and ask if we were married and had children. They seemed to soften immediately they saw a photo of the family of one of the men and they would tell us of their children. In fact, I think they were as lonely as we were. They were just ignorant peasants who had been taught to be brutal by a very harsh system.

In all Eastern countries life is held very cheaply, and in their normal existence before the war these guards must have had a very difficult life in Japan. The discipline in their army was as hard as rock, and a kind-hearted person was soon taught to be brutal. In our services a man caught doing something wrong was paraded into an orderly room and given a grade of punishment to suit his crime — usually he lost his privileges and was confined to barracks. In the Japanese army the culprit was likely to be knocked down and then he had to stand up, spring to attention, bow and wait for more.

There were three grades of private in the Japanese army — one-star, two-star, and three-star. The one and two-star men were raw recruits and could be bashed unmercifully by a three-star private or anyone of higher rank. This punishment on the spot was exercised right up through the NCOs and officers. I have seen junior officers being punished by a senior officer using his sheathed sword. Corporals and higher ranks seemed privileged and carried swords, and a corporal in the Japanese army carried far greater authority than his counterpart in ours.

This method of enforcing discipline was one that engendered fear of anyone of superior rank, but it was a system that got things done. If a

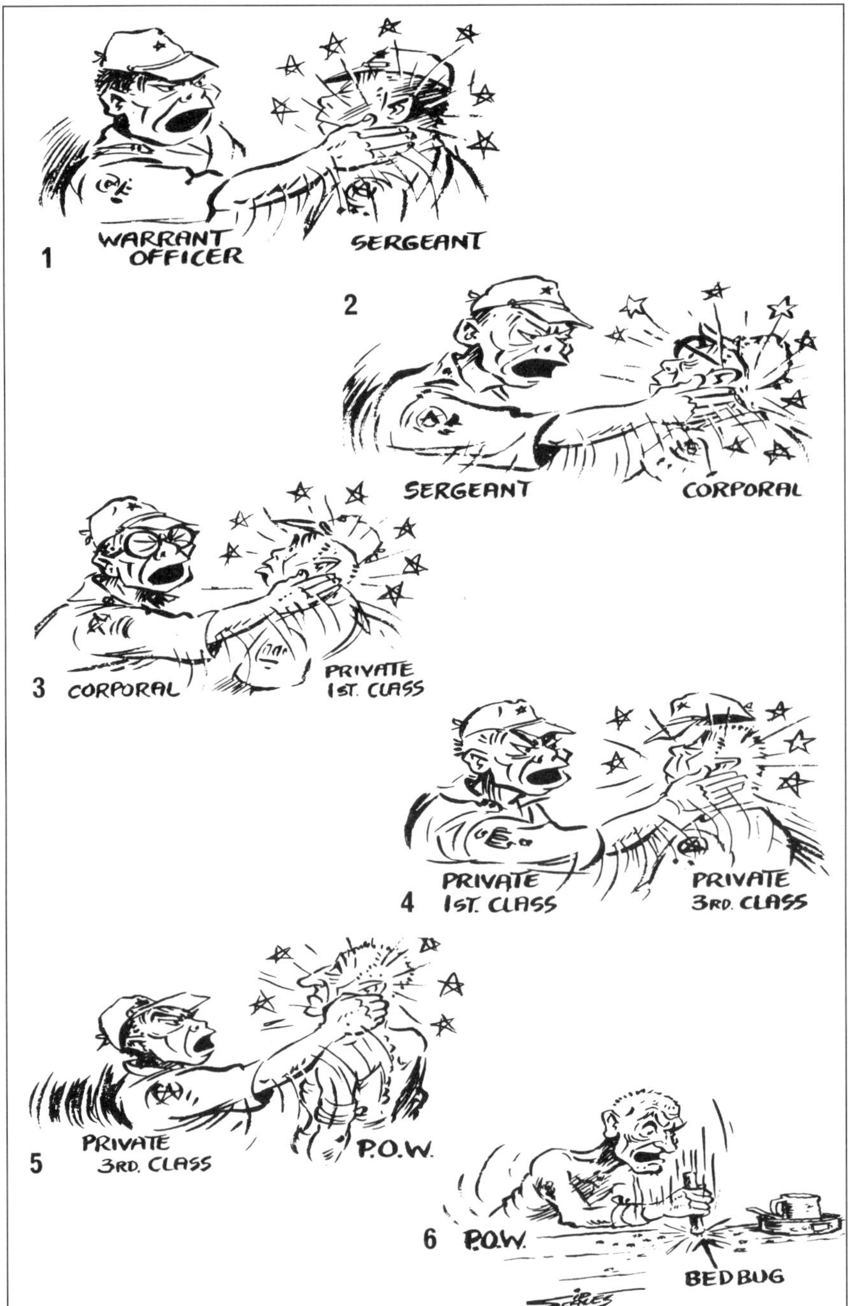

The chain of command in the Greater East Asia Co-Prosperity Sphere.

sergeant had ordered a corporal to see that a certain amount of work was done, the corporal made sure it was done, regardless of how hard and long he worked the POWs, and regardless of the weather or any other cause of delay. To the harassed one- and two-star men we were a heaven-sent opportunity — bashings to be handed out instead of received. Yet I do not think all the bashings were given sadistically. I have received many, and at times I am sure the Jap only thought I was stupid and had made a mistake. When he called me over and tried to tell me I was a fool and shouldn't do such things and I couldn't understand him but just looked dumb, it seemed to unleash some fury in him and in a few moments he would be raining blows on my face.

And Heaven help you if you didn't stand up and take it. If you fell down the torrent of fury seemed to increase and you would be kicked almost insensible. Sometimes after the Jap had cooled down he would try to make amends and offer a gift, such as cigarettes. Some I am sure felt ashamed of losing their tempers so thoroughly. As I write this I am trying to reason from the guard's point of view, and I remember how exasperated I got when I tried to explain some simple thing and the only response was a blank uncomprehending stare. Perhaps a whole library could be written about the psychology of the Japanese at that time. All I can do here is give my impressions of the ones I had to have dealings with — men who I am sure belonged to the lowest social order in Japan.

When I think suddenly of Jaarmarkt now, I don't think of Japs or hardship, but of peanut butter. One happy feature of the Jaarmarkt Camp was a shop inside the camp where we could usually buy some food, if we had money. The greatest luxury for me was to buy peanuts and, after roasting them in a steel helmet, borrow a mincer from an Australian and make peanut butter. A little of this mixed with rice made such a difference that it was a treat I shall never forget.

I wasn't out working all the time in Jaarmarkt. I had malaria two or three times, and while recuperating from these attacks I was able to do some cooking. Another favourite dish that we cooked for ourselves was katyang idjoe (mung beans). They were very small beans about the size of sweet pea seeds and were very nutritious and appetising. The food we prepared ourselves in the cookhouse seemed very tasty and well cooked, and we enjoyed every spoonful, though I suppose that if I had some dished up to me now I wouldn't think it so good. Occasionally we had small rations of native delicacies and we learned to relish these hot dishes. Raw chillies were one of the things we always tried to have in stock.

Tempi was a soya bean dish. The natives soaked soya beans, then left them out in trays until they were covered with mould and flies. When the mould had broken down the hard cellulose skins of the beans, the mess was cut into squares and fried in peanut or coconut oil. It was delicious, as some of my friends know today without being prisoners.

Another native food that was used in most of the stews we had was "Trassie" or, as it was known in Singapore, "blatchen". The smell of a piece of blatchen the size of a finger nail was very strong. It was made from small fish and shrimps which had been caught and then left to rot in great heaps. Villages where trassie was made could be smelt miles away. After the fish had been in these heaps for a time, all the small bones were dissolved, the water gradually oozed out and the rest was then compressed by tramping until it was a solid greyish paste. This, too, was something we came to enjoy very much. It was like good Stilton cheese.

More than half the Dutch at Jaarmarkt were native troops or half-caste Dutch. At this time I was learning Malay and became friendly with some of the Ambonese. These troops held the same reputation for courage and soldiering generally in the Dutch army as the Gurkhas did in the British army. It was from these fine, friendly people that I learned a lot about native cooking.

There was a native dish called a "sambal" — a little of this concoction added to the most unappetising bowl could make it tempting, and often the ingredients made the food of better value. Sometimes up to twelve ingredients would go into a sambal but the important things were always chillies and trassie. The quest for food was now almost our only interest. I didn't seem to be able to read, even though I had the chance at times, and I don't remember football being played at Jaarmarkt.

Chapter 10

VOYAGE TO HARUKU

For a long time I was the only New Zealander in Jaarmarkt. One day a succession of boys came in and said, "You are for it, Tommy. It's been good to know you. So long."

They told me to look on the notice board outside the hut. On the board was a story of the appalling cruelty of the New Zealand people who had mercilessly shot down 67 Japanese POWs for no other reason than to exterminate them. This was the Japanese version of the trouble in a prisoner of war camp in Featherston, New Zealand.* The story on the notice board at Jaarmarkt finished up by describing how the natives of New Zealand, the Maori, had been forced into slavery and were now the white man's slaves.

As a postscript the notice said that reprisals would be carried out against New Zealanders held in Japanese camps. I wondered what would happen. Knowing the camp guards, I knew it was quite likely that they would single out New Zealanders for some special punishment, and I must confess I was quite a bit worried. However, nothing did happen, although for some time I tried to avoid letting the Japanese read the identity card which I, like every other man, always had to wear.

Small parties of fresh POWs were coming into Jaarmarkt at odd times and I was very pleased eventually to find in one of these quite a number

---

*The incident that occurred at Featherston in February 1943 was the subject in 1983 of a memorable play entitled *Shuriken*, by the New Zealand author Vincent O'Sullivan, published by Victoria University Press in 1985. Before writing *Shuriken*, O'Sullivan was able to talk to several of the New Zealand guards, one of the camp's interpreters, and two of the chaplains. From his prefatory note: "Featherston was certainly not a mutiny. Nor was it an attempted outbreak, nor a massacre, nor in any sense an execution. Yet whatever name one chooses to put on it, in less than a minute there were thirty-one Japanese dead, and ninety-one wounded. Nineteen others died over the next few days. There was also one dead New Zealander, and seven injured ... It is difficult to think of two peoples less prepared for each other personally than New Zealanders and Japanese in the 1940s. There had never before been a prisoner-of-war camp for Japanese soldiers, any more than the Imperial military code offered instructions for how prisoners should behave. We had no experience as guards; they had no philosophy to help them cope under arrest."

of New Zealanders. Talking to people from your own country is a very pleasant thing when you have been separated from them for a long time.

Rumours had started again about a move. Some said we'd go to Singapore, some Bandoeng, others hinted at a long voyage. For about three weeks we were kept in suspense. Working parties had been leaving the camp each day and some of them had been sent to the docks to load bombs into the holds of a number of ships. Some thought these ships had something to do with our move.

Finally, about the end of April 1943, we were told we would have to move, and ordered to a medical inspection of the whole camp. We paraded, and were inspected by a Japanese doctor who walked without pause down each rank and declared that we were all fit and well. Actually there were quite a lot of dysentery cases in the camp and our doctor tried to prevent these from going, but many of them had to go.

After the "inspection" we were given a speech by a Japanese major. He told us that we were now in his keeping and that if we did as we were told he would be as a father to us. He said that we were no longer prisoners of ware but part of the glorious Japanese Labour Army. The camp we were going to would be a paradise camp, and all that we would have to do was a little work in return for this good treatment.

From clues contained in the orders about our move, we worked out that we would probably be going somewhere by sea. The popular bet was Japan and we were not keen because remour had it that Dutch and British submarines were sinking much of the Japanese shipping. Still, a move was a move, and it broke the monotony.

Life in the camps had made me quite fatalistic in my outlook. It had appeared to me that it was a good thing just to accept things as they came and not try to alter them. I could possibly have worked it so that I remained in Jaarmarkt if I had pleaded illness, which some did and were left behind with the really sick, but I felt it would be a bad thing to tempt fate.

We left next day, and after marching to the station went by train to the docks. At times of embarkations and moves, the Japanese seemed to work themselves into a frenzy of impatience and excitement. We were beaten and knocked with rifle butts to hurry us on board one of the ships that we had already loaded with bombs. The top of one of the holds of our ship had been allotted to us and we were almost trampled to death getting down the single ladder quickly enough to avoid a rifle butt in the back.

In the hold it was almost completely dark, but after a few moments we were able to see about us. Around the sides of the hold a platform had been built which was about two feet six inches high, and on this and on the entire floor we had to camp.

The first into the hold tried to save a bit of space so that they would have room to sit down in comfort, but the guards came down roaring like madmen and kicked and hammered these people until we were all packed in below. I have no accurate idea of the number of men in our hold but as there were over 4000 of us on the move — 2000 British and 2000 Dutch and officers — and there were four ships, I estimated a good thousand or more, for our ship was the largest. For six days we lay sweating and half suffocated in this dark hold.

One of the ships still loading bombs at the quayside exploded on the second or third day. I was standing near the top of the ladder at the time, and I saw great pieces of smoking timber hurled in the air. Our ship gave a shudder as the blast hit it. At once the Japanese screamed and chased us down the ladder, and closed the hatch completely. What caused the explosion we never knew, but there was a rumour that it was sabotage. It made our quarters feel less secure, for we knew that the hold below us was filled with bombs.

While we were waiting in the harbour a few men were allowed up during the day and we took turns in having a breath of fresh air. The heat was almost unbearable below, and my old friend malaria paid another visit to make things even worse for me. We had rice three times a day and with it some Japanese food that was some kind of seaweed. It was not very palatable, but it helped to fill our stomachs. There were no facilities for washing but we had some showers in the rain. The Japanese treated us exactly as cattle would be treated in New Zealand, and these one or two occasions when we were able to shower in the rain were wonderful.

At last, after six days of waiting, we sailed. We were in a convoy of six ships, four with POWs. Restrictions were relaxed and we were allowed up on deck more often. After sailing for six days we tied up at a wharf in Ambon Harbour. Nothing happened during the rest of the afternoon and we had an uneventful night, but in the morning as some of us were on deck two American planes tried to bomb us, and three anti-aircraft guns started blazing away at them. Again our guards were quite frantic, and we were bundled helterskelter down into the hold with rifle butts helping to hurry us. Fortunately the bombs missed us, and when all was quiet we had to hurry through our meal and clear the centre of the hold so that the winches could unload the cargo below.

The unloading of the ship was utter pandemonium. For two days and two nights we worked in the holds and on the lighters that were being filled. When the hatches were lifted we found that immediately below them were grass sacks full of pomelos — a kind of large citrus fruit — which had rotted during the delay in sailing, and stank to high heaven. Below these were layer upon layer of long lengths of bamboo. In unloading the fruit half of the sacks had broken and the bamboo was covered with a mass of rotten fruit which made it as slippery as glass, and as dangerous to walk on. We had to scoop up this mess in our hands, throw it into unbroken sacks and then dump them overboard. At last it was all finished and the holds were empty but for the bombs.

Early in the morning we sailed out of Ambon and arrived at the island of Ceram. Some of the other ships had come with us and we spent some days unloading bombs, petrol and rice, taking it all by lighter to the shore. Some of us worked in parties on the shore, and we had to wade out into the surf to the lighters, carry the bombs to the beach, up a steep slope, and stack them in a shelter. It was terribly hard work, and we were driven continuously by the guards who were in a frenzy to get the work done. There were very cruel beatings all day long. The Dutch stayed at Ceram, and we heard later that their task was to build an aerodrome. The rest of us, when we had completed the unloading, were all crowded on to a small ship, and off we sailed again.

Chapter 11

HARUKU: WORST CAMP OF ALL

Just before sunset we dropped anchor near an island which at first we could see only dimly through a heavy rain squall. Then suddenly the rain passed and we saw, lit up by the last rays of sunlight, a beautiful tropical island, fringed all around with coconut palms. A long jetty pushed out from the shore and the sea was calm and sheltered. This island we learned later was Haruku, and on it we had to build an aerodrome.

Our short glimpse of the island in sunlight was to be our last for quite a time. Almost immediately the sky clouded over and the island was drenched in rain. The night came suddenly — as it does in the tropics — and we were taken ashore in the very wet darkness. There we stumbled, cursing and swearing, over ground that had but recently been cleared, to a camp that was only half completed. The ground was wet and soggy and we had no dry place to sleep, so we curled up on the wet ground in the shelter of half-finished huts and tried to sleep. As soon as it was light we were hounded down to the beach to unload the ships, and for three days parties worked continuously getting ashore supplies from the ship.

We had only a scanty meal of rice before leaving the ship. Our next meal was about 36 hours later, and it was pap — very watery and with a burnt, smoked taste. To get this we had to queue in the pouring rain for over an hour.

The cooks did a wonderful job, considering the conditions. Brad, the old soldier, had organised himself as a cook but the terrible conditions got him down and he only stayed a few days. I was sorry because a friend in the cookhouse was a friend indeed.

Imagine the difficulties the cooks had to overcome: their cookhouses were not sheltered in any way except by a roof. They had no dry wood. What they had was cut green, and was wet with rain as well. For cooking utensils they had only some large, dish-shaped pans called "wajangs", a few large cans, and petrol tins. To keep the fires burning they had to be fanned continuously. It was a weird sight to see the half-naked cooks sweating about their fires. Their eyes were running and sore for it was

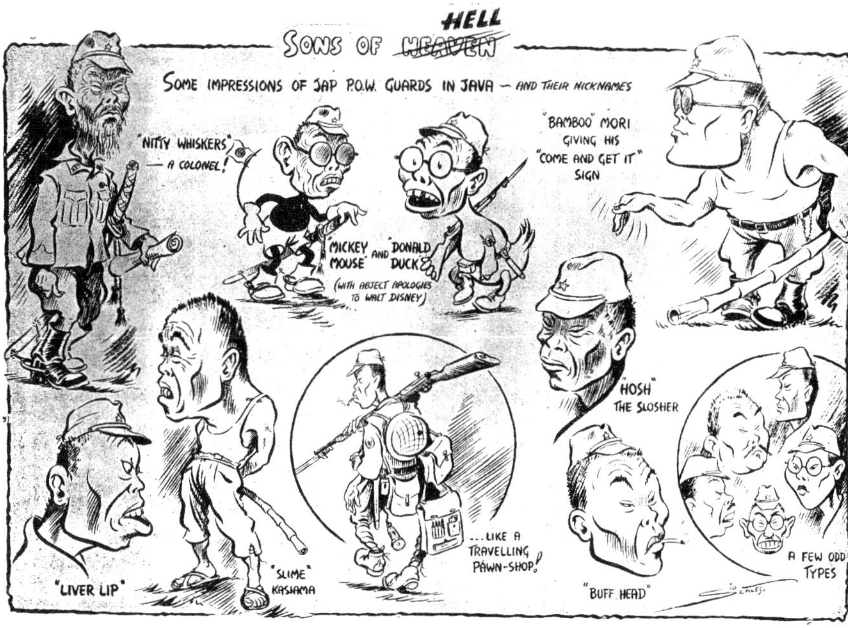

These caricatures are replicas of drawings made in a prisoner-of-war camp in Java by Flight-Lieut. S.E. Scales. The original drawings were hidden in the camp, but because of unsettled conditions it was impossible to recover them. "Nitty Whiskers" represents Colonel Anami, who was notorious for his studied neglect of prisoners ("his children", as he called them) in his charge in Ambon and Java. "Mickey Mouse", another Japanese officer, Kawabe by name, was Anami's right-hand man. "Donald Duck", who was a very bandy third-class private, was more ridiculous than harmful, and he made a pest of himself when in charge of pigs and gardens in a Bandoeng camp. Sergeant "Bamboo" Mori, however, was a much more vicious type who delighted in imitating a gorilla and who wielded a bamboo pole with telling effect. Lower left is "Liver-lip" who was just what he looked — a dumb Japanese private. "Slime" Kasiama, though a private, was far from dumb, being half Jap-anese and half Korean, a combination of little intellect and low cunning. Being adept at setting traps for prisoners and then punishing them in some unusual and painful manner, he was one of the most hated guards. Strange to relate, his proud boast was that he had worked in the YMCA and was a "Clistian". "Hosh the Slosher" (Sgt. Hoshino) was a particularly brutal type, being frequently dangerously drunk and notorious for his mad rages and beatings-up. Even his own officers had no control over him. Another bad type was "Buff-head", a big private who delighted in putting the boot in when his seniors had finished beating some unfortunate prisoner. In the circles in the picture is a little more local colour.

usually impossible to see through the thick smoke across the width of the hut. Later, enough dry wood was procured to keep the fires burning well.

All this time the unloading went on continuously, night and day. Not all of us had to work at night but a large party was always required and men who had worked hard all day had to carry on right through the night. It took about three days and nights to unload all the equipment and stores. When this was finished work slackened, and we had to work during the day only. For about a week we tidied up the camp, and carried bamboo up from the beach for the native carpenters to use on our huts. We were still having to sleep on the ground with only a roof above us and no walls. The sun had deserted us altogether and our clothes were always wet. Sometimes the rain would stop for a while but soon it was pouring down again. These islands have been named the "Rainy Isles", and the name is apt.

On our voyage from Java — in fact before we left Surabaya — some of the men went down with dysentery. These were isolated cases, but after a time at Haruku dysentery really began to spread. The hard work, continuous rain and damp clothing, and of course the poor food, aided by the flies, were responsible. Our latrines were just open trenches dug between the huts. We had to squat on bamboo cases which were laid across these trenches. Not only were they primitive also but filthy, and often during heavy downpours they would overflow. Maggots, carrying, no doubt, the dysentery bug, crawled across the ground and reached the huts.

When work started on the aerodrome the Japanese demanded 1600 men each day. I think the aerodrome was about 2 miles from the camp. What I am sure of is that it was a long march along a track that was covered in mud in most parts to a depth of about 6 inches — in some parts to over a foot.

Our work on the airfield was either shifting earth or cracking rocks. We were now having short spells with no rain during the day, but still there was no sunshine. The meal we were served at the aerodrome was dry rice. After a day's work there and the march back to camp we were completely exhausted. We found on arrival at camp that our evening meal was nearly always delayed, so that we had to wait, sometimes several hours, and then have another long wait in a queue.

After about a fortnight all work on the aerodrome by the POWs stopped, for by this time dysentery had taken complete charge of the camp, and less than a month from our arrival on the island about 1600 men were down with it. First one hut, then others, would be enclosed in a barbed wire fence, until nearly all of the camp was behind barbed wire, and there were only enough fit men to prepare and cook the food and carry it in to the rest, and do essential duties. As quickly as possible the huts were finished, but for a long time sick men in agony had to try to sleep on the damp mud floors.

Dysentery is a foul disease anywhere, but in these conditions it was hellish. Time after time — often from 30 to 50 times a day — the poor sufferers would have to exert all the willpower they possessed, and stagger, often through pouring rain and over slippery, muddy ground, to the latrines, and squat in agony. It was no wonder that many thought the fight for life was not worth the effort, and soon died.

Sometimes the dead amounted to twelve a day, sometimes one or two, but for a long period at Haruku not one day passed without someone being carried to the cemetery. At first the bodies were hurried away in a rough timber coffin, but after a little while only a rough crate of split bamboo was used. The burials took place in the darkness and the bearers were the fit men detailed after their other duties ceased.

At last the weather slowly improved, and the main rush of the disease grew slightly less. Men began to recover but preferred to stay in the hospital area rather than work. Of course this did not suit the Japanese, who wanted their aerodrome constructed. At first they used threats, but that was no use, so they struck at us through our stomachs. They ordered three scales of rations: No.1 scale, for the workers on the drome, was to include all the meat that was available for the camp, and dry cooked rice for every meal; No.2 scale, for workers inside the camp, would be pap for breakfast and dry rice for lunch and dinner with a vegetable soup; No.3 ration for the sick was to be pap for each meal plus a watery soup.

To this hospital diet can be attributed most of the appalling waste of life at Haruku. No one who had been really ill with dysentery could recover on such food. In no time hundreds of the hospital patients had beriberi in its most shocking form.

For the Japanese, however, this system of rationing had the desired effect, and any who had been malingering (really a form of resistance when you are a POW) or anyone who had recovered sufficiently, left the hospital and soon reported for work. In a short time parties of 400 POWs were working on the aerodrome, and on the comparatively good diet they recovered. I knew of this work only by hearsay, for except for two short days I remained in the hospital area from the time I fell sick until I was sent back to Java.

The highlight of my few days' work on the aerodrome was the wonderful kindness of the natives. Each evening as we trudged home we would be given food as we passed through a village between the drome and the camp. The guards always kept a sharp lookout to stop any contact with the natives, but somehow they would get things to us. Usually it was bananas and these we ate immediately because we were sometimes searched as we went back into the camp.

The Japanese were terrified of disease, so we had little interference in the hospital. If they had to come inside they wore gauze pads over their mouths. They were very concerned if anyone from the hospital tried to get into the other part of the camp. It was considered a great crime, and the wrongdoers were severely punished. Some of the hospital huts were almost on the beach and for a time those POWs who were well enough washed their dishes and bathed in the sea, but the guards stopped this after a while because they thought the sea would be a carrier of the disease. They used to swim a little further along the coast and they thought they might become infected. Later we were allowed to bathe, but not to wash our dishes in the sea. One day a Japanese doctor and orderlies arrived [all orderlies in all camps were prisoners of war] and all the patients who were up were given a humiliating dysentery test. One by one we were herded into a small hut. We had to drop our shorts and bend over while a Jap roughly inserted a piece of bamboo. This was smeared on a slide and then carefully numbered and packed away. We never heard the result of these tests.

Chapter 12

HARUKU HOSPITAL

The most popular officer in the camp was a New Zealander, Flying Officer D.C. Duff.* He was from somewhere in the South Island, perhaps Dunedin. He was allowed by the Japs to visit us and spent his time and money visiting the huts and doing what he could for the sick men. Later he took charge of the kits of the men who died. To "Duffy" and one other, a medical orderly, I probably owe my life. Duffy brought me extra food in the form of dried fish and bananas. Only those who were fortunate enough to get extra food could survive.

The senior doctor was a very fine man, a clever Dutch surgeon named Springer, who worked long hours doing whatever he could. I came to know him very well. One day on his rounds he said to me, with feeling in his voice, "If only we had a little nutritious food we could save all these lives." But the food and medicines he needed never came, and he suffered mental tortures in not being able to cure his patients. He used an ordinary razor to perform amazing operations. These were conducted in the open under a mosquito net. We were lucky, too, in having a good dentist with us. He did a root filling in one of my teeth and extracted another — without anaesthetic.

The camp at Haruku was built on a nutmeg plantation. Among the nutmeg trees were some coconut palms and some huge camairy or candle nut trees. Some of the huts were built around these trees, the tops of the trees sticking out of the roofs. Quite a lot of coconut palms had buildings around them in this way and it was not uncommon for heavy coconuts to come crashing through the roofs of the huts. No one was seriously hurt this way, but there were some near misses. A direct hit would certainly crack a skull since a green coconut weighs 9 pounds. There was always a scramble for a fallen one as a coconut was a prize indeed.

---

*Flying Officer Donald Duff, who was with the R.A.F. in Singapore, was born in Lyttelton in 1910 and spent most of his life in the South Island of New Zealand as a government servant. From a senior position after the war he was seconded for a time to the government of Malaysia.

We had plenty of nutmeg and mace with which to flavour our pap. A nutmeg tree yields two foods in one. Its fruit is about the size of an apricot, and it has about the same amount of flesh covering its kernel, which is the nutmeg. The flesh, however, is astringent, and not edible. The nutmeg kernel is separated from the flesh by a layer of petals which are the mace. This is sold as a separate spice. The camairy nuts, too, had a very rich kernel, but with a shell too hard to crack except with a hammer, and to do even that was difficult. To make a candle a sharp corner of the nut was knocked off, and that would be lit and burn for some time.

In the hospital there was no laughter, and little conversation of any kind. The one thing we talked about was food. The most popular pastime was the working out and printing of elaborate menus, and the collecting and recording of recipes. Day after day men worked on them and then wrote them down until paper supplies dwindled. Smoking was the greatest relief we had. I am sure that many more would have died but for the solace of tobacco. I cannot remember any POW who didn't smoke after a time. The tobacco at Haruku was the vilest and strongest that I experienced. I had to give it two washings in salt water and a final rinse in weak tea (which was our only fresh water ration) before I could smoke the stuff.

If no tobacco was available we tried dried pawpaw leaves, tea leaves and banana leaves. Paper was scarce and we wrapped our cigarettes in anything we could get. Usually we did as the natives did and wrapped them in leaves of a shrub, which gave them a peculiar flavour. We used the leaves quite green and had to keep puffing to keep them alight.

After I reported sick I was sent into the hospital and had to lie in an unfinished hut. When I arrived I found that only about six other people were sharing it with me. I picked the driest piece of ground I could find and tried to sleep. We were entirely neglected, and kept alternately staggering out to the latrines and trying to sleep. By the end of the next day our hut was full of violently ill men. Most of them never said a word but just endured their pain quietly. Others screamed and screamed that they did not want to die.

The stench of a hut full of men suffering from dysentery who have no means of cleaning themselves properly is something that has to be experienced to be believed. I do not know how long I was in this hut, and am only dimly aware of a lot that happened. I remember one of the men, a very decent chap, going mad and trying to break out of the hut to join the Aussies who, he imagined, had just landed. I also remember that he and quite a few others died. Fortunately for me I was very fit before I was captured, and I recovered. When I was considered no longer a serious case I was moved to another hut to recuperate.

In this hut conditions were much better. Being with men who are not so ill is a great help to recovery, and after about three weeks I was well enough to leave the hospital and do some light work in the camp. But malaria struck again and I had to go back to hospital. The malaria weakened me so much that I was an easy victim for a return of dysentery, and I was returned to Hut 3 where serious cases were housed.

Huts 1, 2 and 3 were supervised personally by Dr Springer. My case was now considered serious; I could eat no food, and was rapidly losing strength. I was content just to lie back on my bamboo bench between trips to the latrine. I found that the thought of dying — and I knew I was close to it — did not alarm me. I was just too weak to care.

Just at this time a medical orderly whom I had got to know well — we were members of the same lodge — must have heard of my condition and, though working in another part of the camp, he came during the night and secretly gave me two sulpha tablets. How he got them I do not know; they were beyond price in the camp. Almost immediately the dysentery was cleared up, but I was still very weak and had bad beriberi. The dysentery had affected my stomach, and even though there was no infection I could not digest the food, but had a continued enteritis. It was at this time that Duffy looked after me with extra food that was easily digested. I still did not progress as I should have done and one day Dr Springer told me that I was to be moved to Hut 2.

To be moved to either Hut 1 or 2 was almost like a death sentence for the majority, for it was here that the hopeless cases were sent, and not many recovered. My fear of Huts 1 and 2 must have shown on my face for Dr Springer quickly reassured me that in my case it was not because I was going to die but so that I could have the benefit of the slightly better food.

Chapter 13

YOGA AT THE MORGUE

I cannot describe conditions in Hut 2. I think that if some perfectly healthy person direct from one of our cities had suddenly been installed in Hut 2 he would not have lived long. We had become gradually adapted to horrible conditions and could take a lot, but Hut 2 was shocking to me. Fortunately, I was allotted a space at the best end of the hut where the men who were not so sick were installed, but even so, the sights were terrible. Only about three of us were able to go to the latrines. Most of the others were too weak even to sit up, and were prostrate on sacks spread over bamboo platforms.

The orderlies did a great job for these sick men. In Hut 2 there were about 80 to 100 patients, and all day and night the orderlies fed, panned and washed them amid groans and cries. Most of these patients had practically no control over their bowels and the hut reeked with the stench of bacillary dysentery. At this time planes were bombing Ambon which was only about 30 or 40 miles away, and at night if there was an air raid alarm all lights had to be extinguished and could not be relit until the Japanese gave permission. Either they forgot to do this or the raids lasted a long time. When this happened the orderlies had to cease work and all night long the poor patients had to lie in their excreta.

These raids were now quite frequent. Sometimes we heard the planes and at others a warning must have been relayed to the Japs. One day we saw a formation of three large planes, and from them as we watched there streamed a shower of silver. They were dropping leaflets but none fell in the camp.

Time meant very little to me during this period and I do not know how long I stayed in Hut 2, but I expect it would be from three weeks to a month. During that time in the space on my right five or six men died. Death, like everything else, is something you get used to and we did not worry much. Our chief emotion was a keenness to share the dead man's food if his ration had not been stopped in time for the next meal.

The personal effects of the dead men were immediately locked up and later given over to Duffy's charge. Anything of personal value was parcelled up and handed to the Japanese to send to the Red Cross. Articles of clothing, blankets and eating utensils were distributed to the people in the camp who were most in need of them. Duffy had an unenviable job to distribute these fairly, for any article had a value and was sought after by crowds of POWs.

The food in the hut was the lightest in the whole camp — just pap and a clear soup strained of solids, but with extra bananas which we could eat after they were thoroughly mashed. Each day in both Huts 2 and 3 I was requested by the doctor to show him a sample which I wrapped in a leaf. After about a month he said he would send me to Hut 4 to see if I could manage the normal hospital fare which was different only in the amount and coarseness of the soup. But my stomach could stand only a day in Hut 4 and I was moved back, this time to Hut 1.

Hut 1, like Hut 3, was right on the beach. It was a hut in which men were dying all the time, but was divided into two parts. At one end were the dying cases, and divided by a partition was a ward for people like myself, who needed the lighter food but could do a lot for themselves. After my relapse I improved steadily and was fairly contented in these surroundings. In time I was able to walk slowly to the beach and have a quiet bathe. If I exercised too violently or walked too far I immediately had a relapse, and my trips to the latrine increased from seven or eight times a day to about twenty.

I managed to read a few books, and one of them was about yoga. This I studied and for a time tried to practise some of the elementary parts. Quietness away from people was essential, and a problem, until Duffy gave me the use of a small room attached to the morgue which was at the end of our hut. In this room Duffy stored dead men's clothing and effects which had to be boiled before distribution. I used to sneak into the room using a key he lent me and, sitting crosslegged in the correct fashion, I tried to do the breathing and meditation exercises. I think they helped me quite a lot.

For anyone who could forget the squalor and misery on Haruku there was beauty to enjoy in abundance. The sparkling calm sea with its wonderfully coloured coral was a joy to look at. Sunsets were breathtakingly lovely, but few saw them. I did, and I am sure that the enjoyment I had from the beauty helped me greatly. Coconut palms in the moonlight, fireflies completely outlining a huge camairy tree at night, and the view across the water to the island of Ceram all left lasting impressions on me.

In Hut 1 I tried engraving, with a sharp steel point, the aluminium utensils I used for food. Duffy had acquired for me a set of Dutch utensils. I engraved my Japanese name and number on a small square of aluminium and was very pleased with the result. Simple things satisfied us. I think we were all not quite normal on Haruku.

After we had been on the island for about seven months, rumours again started up about a move for some of us, and as usual they were based on fact. Seven hundred of the sick were to be sent back to Java. With great feelings of thankfulness I found I was one of those going back. Up to the time I left the island there had been 367 deaths. Duffy, whose job it was to keep official records, used to keep telling me the total. Somehow the immensity of the death roll did not impress me greatly until, for the first time for about six months, I was walking down to the jetty and I passed the camp cemetery. The sight of row upon row of graves in a clearing gave me a shock and impressed upon me the enormous amount of wasted life. Three hundred and sixty-seven out of a total of 2000 comparatively fit men died, and 700 human wrecks were on the way to Java. All this happened in a few months, and still the camp was working, and many more were to die before the aerodrome was finished.

I have not said much about the Japanese on Haruku. We were in charge of some quite notorious men, and at least three of them were executed promptly after the war. The head man was the major we called Bluebeard, who lived for the most part in Ambon. He left the running of the camp to a Warrant Officer whom we called Bamboo Mori. The name was very apt for he always carried a heavy piece of bamboo and broke it more often than not every day over some poor POWs back. In any country's army Mori would have been a good soldier because he was a great disciplinarian and a good organiser, but he was ruthless towards the prisoners when they stopped working. He wore tinted spectacles, and the rumour was that he was in the secondary stage of syphilis. He was a very big Jap and as strong as an ox.

Wherever Bamboo Mori went he was accompanied by the Japanese interpreter Kasuyama. Kasuyama was a very nasty type and we never trusted him. He proudly called himself a Christian, but he failed to impress us with his virtue. We feared Mori for his ruthlessness but we understood him and could at least trust him to behave in a particular way. Kasiyama was not worthy even of that trust and least of all when he was telling us — as he often did — of the good he was doing for us. We called the two men Blood and Slime.

Another bad type was an N.CO whom we called Yellow Boots. He had a mad look in his eye, and we feared him greatly. It was Yellow Boots who, on one of the boats returning to Java, found one of the POWs on deck and in a mad fury literally cut off the prisoner's head.

No other Japanese stand out in my memory of Haruku. They were just Japs, but because of the conditions they became more callous than before. I should think that most of them hated this island as we did, for although their living conditions were infinitely better than ours, they were not as well off as they had been in Java.

One of our men was killed on the aerodrome by a truck backing over him. The Japs made a great show of his funeral because he had died working for Nippon. The CO and most of the Japanese turned out for this funeral, and the camp carpenter had to make a proper coffin.

At Haruku the Japanese had some kind of service each morning. Since it took place down by the jetty we could hear them chanting in unison. I would have liked to see them but I never had the chance. Chanting was also heard at night, but this was from the native fishermen as they fished out in the sea. It must have been part of their usual fishing routine for we heard them nearly every night chanting in time with a regular beating of some sort of drum. These chants sounded very Christian, and could possibly have been so, as this was one of the very early mission stations which had been established by Portuguese missionaries.

Chapter 14

AWAY FROM HARUKU

We were given about 24 hours' notice to move, and spent the day packing our scanty gear and saying cheerio to those who were remaining. My gear was a set of three Dutch dixies on which I had engraved tikis, palm trees and even a view of the island Ceram; the battle dress given to me by the wedana at Manondjaja; khaki shorts and shirt, a torn groundsheet, and my blanket and sarong. Not a large pack, fortunately, for in my weak state I could not have managed anything more.

Early on the following morning we were issued with our day's ration of food. We were then paraded, and counted again and again until the Japanese were sure that the right number of bodies was present, and then we were marched down to the jetty. It was on this march that I saw for the first time the camp graveyard, where the row after row of crosses awoke in me a realisation of how many deaths there had been on Haruku. The graves were well kept, for the Japs seemed to respect the dead in this way. Nearby was the grave of a Japanese who had died, and this was a most elaborate affair.

Why we were taken to the jetty so early in the day I have no idea, for we had a long, long wait in the sun, while the hundred or more stretcher cases were carried on board. Not all of the very sick were coming back to Java with us. The doctors had the awful responsibility of leaving all those men whom they considered would not withstand the trials of the journey and a great number were left to die. Late in the afternoon we boarded the ship. Fortunately I was one of the last on board and, as there was no room below, I had to stay on deck. The Japanese idea of a full hold was one that could hold no more people standing. No allowances were made for people sleeping. The heat under these conditions was unbearable, for the hatches were down and only a small opening was left where the ladder went down into the hold.

No stretcher cases were in the hold. These were laid over the hatches and on any clear space on the deck. The rest of us were crowded wherever there was standing room. Until the sun went down it was very hot on deck, but I congratulated myself on my luck in not being one of the unfortunates in the hold or one of the helpless stretcher cases, either.

Accompanying the sick was a party of about 50 fit men to see to their luggage, to help carry them, and to serve them in any way possible. Also there were a few orderlies and one Dutch doctor. About half the sick were beriberi cases and the rest had dysentery. The very sick dysentery ones were having to call for a pan up to 50 times a day, and the least sick ones never under about six or seven times.

In our primitive hospital huts the orderlies had developed quite a system, but on ship this broke down and orderlies had a hectic time trying to aid all these helpless men. They had only about four half kerosene tins for pans, and about a dozen bamboos for use as urinals. These bamboos were about a foot long and had an internal diameter of about 2 inches. The bamboo was cut so that one end was open and the other closed by being cut below a joint.

For those of us who were fit enough there was a plank protruding through a scupper on the side of the ship. To use this latrine you had to climb over the ship's side, holding firmly on to the rail, and place your feet on the plank. Fortunately, the sea in this area is usually calm or it would have been impossible in our weakened condition to perform this antic.

It was dark when everything had been loaded and we left the jetty and dropped anchor a short way out from shore. It is quite an ordeal for a fit person to stand up all night. To us it was hell. We were really hungry, too, for our ration of food had all gone quickly during the day. It had been dry rice instead of pap and was the best food we had received for many months. It was soon only a memory, and we spent a very miserable night, but fortunately it did not rain. Just before daybreak we set course.

From Haruku direct to Ambon was only about 30 miles. Haruku was a beautiful sight as we left it in the dawn, but probably very few realised it. All were thankful that at last we were leaving a hell spot and felt that now our chances of survival would be increased, for we were sure that we were headed for Java, and that in a few days, probably six at the most, we would arrive in that land of comparative plenty. As soon as the ship started to move the morale of the whole crowd was boosted, for there is nothing that depresses you more than waiting to move.

Our trip to Ambon was quite uneventful except that an American Flying Fortress bombed us as we were entering the harbour. You feel large and vulnerable enough at any time when bombs are being dropped, but on the crowded deck of a small ship you are helpless. To make matters worse the Japanese turned their anti-aircraft machine guns on to us and said, through an interpreter, that if anyone panicked in any way, they'd fire. It was a very tense few minutes, but in that time I noticed that the Japanese sailors seemed to be indifferent to the threat of a bomb hitting the ship, and went about their duties as if it was a perfectly normal thing. I was amused to compare them with our Korean guards, who were terrified. Luckily, when the bombs did drop they missed us, and fell on the shore a few hundred yards away.

Our small ship, after the bombs had dropped, stopped its avoiding action and moved across to a large ship that was obviously being used as a troop transport: there were planks pushed through the scuppers for use as latrines. When we reached her we manoeuvred alongside and tied up. Almost immediately a gangplank was lowered, and amidst the usual pandemonium that marked all embarkation and disembarkation of POWs, some of the men were driven like animals up on to the larger ship. Then something changed their plans, and amid great shouting and obvious consternation the gangplank was raised, our ship cast off, and we moved to another part of the harbour to wait.

As we left the side of the larger ship we saw boatloads of Japanese arriving at the ship, and we heard that our places were taken by Japanese wounded in our air raids.

Ambon is a very lovely, and very good harbour. It was formerly a Dutch naval base. A great number of Australian POWs were working at Ambon and they had a very bad time. We still had all the stretcher cases covering the hatches and deck, but the hold was not so crowded and the number of people standing on deck had decreased, so that it was possible to sit down. We waited all day in the scorching sun in the land-locked harbour and received no food or drink. A few of us had water bottles, but only a few. Toward sunset the large ship sailed and we all felt very disappointed at having to stay.

"Look at those lucky hounds. They'll be in Java in about four days," was the general comment; we thought ourselves very unfortunate, but we learned much later that their ship had been torpedoed and no one was saved.

Before long it began to rain. For almost three hours it poured down as it can only in the tropics. No wind, just rain pouring solidly out of the skies, with lightning flashing and thunder almost deafening us. In a few minutes all on deck were soaked. There was no shelter of any kind. Some of those on deck tried to crowd into the hold, but only a few found room, for tired men who had been standing down there all night had quickly taken any spare room made available when the two hundred went aboard the other ship.

The poor devils who were helpless on stretchers had the worst time of all. They had no shelter and couldn't move. In a few minutes they were wet through and cold. The change of temperature was probably not very great, but to bodies that were weak and used to heat the change was frightful. In this solid mass of falling water lit only by lightning flashes the orderlies could not cope with their job. The cold, too, increased the need for pans, and soon excreta was dripping through the cracks between the planks forming the hatches onto those below.

Those who were at the sides of the hold were all right, but those in the centre who were on the piles of luggage — and the luggage itself — were covered. I expected that few of the stretcher cases would survive the night, but some men have great endurance and will to live, and we found that only about five had died. They were buried at Ambon, and a lot of those still living but very sick were taken ashore. A small amount of food came out to the ship at about midday, but it was badly apportioned and some men received none at all.

After being chilled all night we were roasted all day. We seemed to have been forgotten, and spent the following night in the same positions. This night was cold, and we could not sleep on the cold steel deck, but it wasn't wet, and for this we were grateful.

Chapter 15

TRAVEL WITH NIPPON

Late the following afternoon our ship weighed anchor and we moved across the harbour alongside a small tramp steamer of about 6–7000 tons. Once again the Japs went mad as we were transferring from one ship to another and all of us, the sick and very sick, were buffeted and shoved up a steep gangplank and then down a vertical ladder into two holds of the ship. It was evening when we were transferred, and though on deck it was light, down in the hold it was almost pitch dark even with the hatch covers off. We hoped that they would stay off but they were only off because the stretcher cases had to be lowered from above. As soon as they were all below the hatches were replaced and we were in total darkness. In our hold were all the dysentery cases, and in the other hold the beriberi cases and others, the numbers being roughly equal, 200 men in each hold.

Of what happened in the other hold I have no knowledge, but the dysentery hold I shall never forget. The floor space was not enough to allow all to lie down. By crowding body against body there was space for about half to lie and the others to sit. It was impossible to be comfortable; you could not turn when your limbs were lying across someone else's.

In the confusion and haste when the Japanese had beaten and shoved us below we had not had time to become organised at all, and the sick and near dying were scattered all over the hold. Because it was so dark nobody could see a thing, and as no attempt had been made to form narrow passages down which the orderlies could shuffle with their pans and bamboos, the filth and squalor of that night was indescribable. Utterly worn-out men, with probably their first chance to sleep for about three days, were scattered amongst these men who had need of the orderlies twice an hour. A voice would come from nowhere in the darkness screaming for a pan and the orderlies would be struggling to locate that voice, fumbling with their feet to avoid walking on bodies, all the while carrying a sawn-off kerosene tin probably half full already because it was a difficult journey to empty it over the side.

Imagine the state of mind of the men who were being repeatedly walked on. In all my experiences I have never known a night of such swearing and cursing from men who had just about reached the limit. If they were walked on they either struck out or pushed, frightened that someone was going to usurp their small amount of space. Time and time again the orderlies fell, and with them their stinking burden, until a large portion of the hold was covered in slime, and the whole place reeked with this terrible dysentery stench which is the vilest of smells. We had by this time become so accustomed to horrible conditions that we survived these, but had we come straight from civil life I doubt that we would have. The heat was oppressive, for the only ventilation was a small square where the ladder reached the deck. We envied the orderlies, who were able to go on deck to empty their cans and bamboos.

In the morning a couple of planks were removed from the hatches, and a feeble light penetrated below. Some of our party of 50 fit boys did the removing of the planks and, recoiling visibly from the stench that rose from below, they refused to come down and help clean up. So it rested with ourselves and the orderlies to try to clean up our quarters, and to organise sanitary arrangements. All the very sick were placed in the centre where the orderlies could minister to their wants, and although it cut down the sleeping space, narrow paths amongst the bodies were formed so that others who wanted the orderlies could be reached.

The Japs were approached and they granted a concession that any who were able to climb the ladder might go up on deck and use a latrine that was rigged up over the side. This was a concession indeed if one was fit enough, but only a few were able to use it. It was a concession not to be abused, too, for the condition was that there was to be no loitering on deck. It became a very sought-after privilege, but we always kept the queue below, and allowed only one person on deck to wait his turn to climb over the side of the ship on to the plank. Luckily the seas in this area were calm or we couldn't have used these latrines after sailing.

The heat was a great trial. The nights were not so bad, but the days were torture. There was practically no wind, for we were in a land-locked harbour. We were also almost on the equator and, worst of all, crowded into a small space with insufficient ventilation. Under these conditions it is natural that we needed a great deal to drink to replace the fluid lost. Our ration of tea was the only water we received, and this was a half-pint mug in the morning at about 10 a.m. and a similar one about 5 p.m.

The food ration was the smallest amount that I had received as a regular ration. It was a half-pint of thick pap in which was a little Jap seaweed food, which we received just before our tea in the morning and again at five, but then the seaweed was replaced by a few tiny, hard, black fish. The food was sent down to us in wooden tubs and a strict watch was kept as it was served out to see that no one received more than his correct share. If, after each had received his half-pint, a little remained, it would be given in half measures as extra to groups of POWs in order, and their names crossed off the list. Also working from the end of the list a roster was kept for the privilege of scraping the already well-scraped tubs. Food was always our most pressing thought as POWs, but here was added the torture of thirst.

Each day we hoped we would move, but the engines lay still. We wondered how we could endure another day, but each one passed and nothing happened. A week went by and the only change in our routine was that just once a day for about half an hour those who could crawl up the ladder on to the deck would be sprayed with salt water from the ship's hoses. This was a great treat and those who were able to reach the deck revelled in the cool, splashing water. For myself this shower was something I enjoyed almost as much as the food. A few of us discovered that at times the draincocks for the winches would supply a small quantity of rather rusty, oily water, and this we quickly drank.

It seemed incredible that we all survived, for after ten days we were still in the harbour waiting to move. Our bodies were oily with the fluid we were exuding in place of sweat. We were thinner than ever, and when not on deck for a shower just sat and tried to stretch out and rest. The seemingly endless waiting affected the morale of the POWs and we wondered if we would ever move. One good event happened. We were allowed up on deck during a terrific rain storm, and we were able to replenish our water bottles and drink until we almost burst. One or two died during this time, and were buried in Ambon.

The condition of us all seemed to be getting worse, and fewer and fewer were able to crawl on deck to be showered, while more relied on the orderlies with their pans. What would have happened if we had had to stay much longer I cannot say, but I think that most had reached their limits of endurance when, after 18 days of waiting and sweating in Ambon, we sailed.

It was a great boost to morale, and although our conditions never altered, the spirits of the men rose. The moving ship created a small breeze and life was a little better. The ship stopped twice, at Celebes and at Borneo. They were short stops, and seven days after leaving Ambon we arrived back at Java, at Surabaya early in the afternoon. Once again the Japs behaved as if they were mad, and drove us up from the holds and down rope ladders to the dock. The poor ones, too weak to do this, were dumped in rope nets, swung out and lowered over the side to the dock. As soon as the net was raised all were thrown in a heap in the centre, which was quite a delight to the Japs. Those on stretchers were treated in the same way, and when lifted the stretchers and men were all tumbled on top of one another. Watching, I realised my good fortune in being able to crawl down the ladder.

Before we disembarked we had been issued with our morning meal and wondered if we would have our evening one. We didn't. No food arrived. Instead we were paraded and the really sick were laid out on the wharves and counted. Slowly it became dark, and we soon realised that we must spend the night in the open. The whole trip took 28 or 29 days from when we left Haruku until we arrived in Surabaya. It should have taken five or six.

Chapter 16

ONE GOOD MEAL

It rained heavily during this first night in Surabaya, and although an empty shed was behind us we were not allowed to enter it. We spent a very miserable night. Next morning no food arrived and this was serious, because we had missed our meal the night before. We were hounded into some railway carriages that were in a siding behind the wharf. Then began another long wait, and soon the crowded carriages were like ovens.

About midday we were issued with tiny loaves. These loaves were only slightly larger than small muffins, but made in the standard bread shape to look like miniature loaves. Their size was roughly three inches by two inches. After the endless pap they were delicious, but insufficient. Nevertheless, we were lucky to be issued with them three times a day. We were very thirsty, and though there was a water tap quite near, and some of us filled our dixies and water bottles, the guard went mad at us and no others were allowed to fill theirs.

Whenever I think of lice, I think of Surabaya and that railway carriage. We were probably not more infested than usual but I remember taking off my shorts and shirt and systematically going along the seams killing lice. Even now the thought of a bite from a louse seems to affect my nerves and put me on edge.

That night our carriages were hitched on behind a train and we went roaring through the darkness towards the west. We had a few stops during the night, and each time, before we came to a standstill, all shutters had to be lowered so that no one could see out. Just as the dawn was breaking we pulled into Cheribon, a large town on the Javan coast. Of course we could see nothing. Suddenly we were ordered to open the shutters and the first thing I saw was a native ladling tea out of a bucket. Quickly my dixies were out the window, filled, and each of the few boys around me quenched his thirst. We then looked about the platform hoping that some sort of a meal had been prepared for us, but saw no sign of food. Apart from our native tea man, some railwaymen and some Japs, the platform was deserted.

We noticed at last a very large pile of plaited grass boxes, all much the same size — about 9 inches by 6 inches by 2 inches. When someone suggested food we scoffed, but we were wrong. Soon a Japanese shouted for the fit men and they were ordered to distribute the boxes amongst us. We had conjectured from the size of the boxes that three or four people would have to share a box, but to our great joy each POW was issued with one. I have no words to describe our thoughts and reactions during and after this wonderful meal. For months and months we had been slowly starving at Haruku. On our month's journey we had suffered hell in a great number of forms, but by one gesture a great deal of the memory of it was wiped out, for the feast contained in one small box was nothing short of miraculous to us.

About half the box was beautifully dry cooked white rice, and the other half was a mixture of all the nicest native foods. Curried meats, fried banana, hard-boiled egg, fried egg, salted fish, tempi — these were just some of the wonderful assortment. This was probably as good a meal as I had ever had in captivity, and coming at the time it did it remains unforgettable. We were each issued as well with a large orange and a banana.

Actually, these boxes of food were prepared and sold cheaply for the native workmen, and at the time we envied them meals such as this. Unfortunately, not all the sick could enjoy the good food, and some were able to eat only a few mouthfuls. I ate every grain of rice and every piece of food but I must confess that I couldn't have managed any more.

All the time we had been feasting the train had been roaring towards Batavia (now Djakarta), and at about noon we arrived at a station in that city. We wondered what was going to happen to us but didn't much care as long as we could get somewhere to sleep. The food in our stomachs had induced a temporary feeling of contentment. It seemed strange that one reasonable meal could make such a difference.

Our windows had been closed during our run through the suburbs, but we were allowed to open them at the station. Except for some high-ranking Japanese officers and the train crew the station seemed deserted. Later we found that all the streets running to and through the station had been cordoned off from the public. Our guards went quite berserk, in their usual fashion, and we were driven hurriedly out of the train and ordered to parade and be counted. The harsh treatment and blows we received while being hurried on parade were noticed by the Japanese officers and stopped at once. I was quite close to them, and I am sure that

I saw on their faces concern and horror at the condition of the men. We waited about for quite a while, and then an army of trucks arrived to take us to camp.

Those of us who were fit enough to walk were allowed to wander quietly through a deserted street to the camp which was only a short distance away, and was called "Bicycle Camp". It was with great emotion that we trudged through the camp gates, and saw a well-kept camp and well-looked after POWs silently watching us from behind the wire. In most of the faces I read consternation and pity and perhaps a little fear, perhaps feeling that if the Japs could reduce us to our present state their own turn could come.

Chapter 17

BICYCLE CAMP

Bicycle Camp received its name because a battalion of native troops who used bicycles was barracked there. At first we were not allowed to see much of the large camp for we were placed in quarantine by the Japanese, and contact with the other POWs was prohibited. While we waited to be counted food was served to us and we were assured that it was only the usual camp fare. It was very luxurious indeed. Nearby I spotted a water tap, and as soon as I had finished my meal I wandered towards it without attracting anyone's attention and tried it out. To my surprise, not only was it working, but instead of cold water, out flowed lovely hot water, at just the right temperature for a wash.

"Hi you chaps, it's hot water on tap," I yelled, but my remark was greeted with, "Don't be stupid ... what do you think this is, a hotel?" The water immediately attracted quite a few people and there were exclamations and shouts back to their friends.

"The Kiwi is right, chaps!"

We found that Bicycle Camp was built on the site of hot mineral springs and that there was plenty of hot water for washing and bathing.

After quite a wait we were counted again and then searched. All our gear was opened and strewn over the parade ground and the Japanese systematically went through it all. The main concern seemed to be pencils and paper. All books were taken as well. We thought that it was probably the usual procedure here at Bicycle Camp, but found out later that the search was carried out all over the camp and the other camps in the Batavia area. I think the terrible condition in which we arrived in Batavia had shocked the Japanese officers at the station, and the confiscation of all paper and pencils was intended to prevent the story from leaving the camp.

All the buildings at Bicycle were permanent ones, with tiled roofs, concrete walls and paved floors. We were fairly crowded, but apart from having to sleep on the tiles, conditions were quite good. Certainly we all thought that to get back to Java and to a camp such as this was the very best of Christmas presents.

When, after being in quarantine for quite a long while, we were allowed to see the rest of the camp, we found that it was a series of courtyards enclosed by the barrack rooms and other buildings, such as stores and cookhouses. A central road divided the camp into two, and from this road access was gained to each courtyard.

In our courtyard during quarantine a barbed wire fence ran across the square, and we were divided by it from the hospital which was in the rooms surrounding the other part of the square of ground.

For us to try to speak to anyone was forbidden, and those outside were forbidden to speak to us. The only way it could be done secretly was for one of the boys outside to come through the hospital and speak through the wire fence.

Some Aussies did this, and enquired for any of their countrymen. When told that there were no Aussies but one Kiwi, I was called to the wire to speak to them. It had to be done very carefully for the Japanese guard at the gate commanded a view of the wire, but by waiting until he moved away we managed a short talk. Later that evening I had the great thrill of meeting some of the boys from my old Vildebeeste squadron, and from them I learned that some had gone to Japan, some to Singapore and some to the Burma–Thailand railway job. There were three of my old comrades and they brought me some food for Christmas. I considered myself the luckiest man in the world for, apart from extra bread and peanut butter they had brought me undreamed of luxury — a tin of bully beef, and a tin of condensed milk. These three were Jimmy Valentine, a New Zealand pilot, and Jack Green and Doug Cummings, two Aussies.

The second day at camp was spent in washing and organising ourselves into our new home. British doctors came over and inspected us. They promised to see the Japanese authorities about extra medicines, and about having the worst cases admitted to the camp hospital. The Japs made a sudden entry that afternoon, and again searched our belongings for pencils and paper. Some were found, and there was an angry scene with our officer in charge. The Japanese then agreed to leave (probably because of our condition) but they said that any piece of paper or pencil should be voluntarily placed in a pile within a time limit of one hour and then they would be back to search again. If any were found there would be trouble.

Heralded by much "Kyotsky! Kiri! Yesame!" a formidable party of Japs arrived after the time limit had expired. We were all ordered out of the rooms, and for almost an hour we waited, fearful that some silly POW had not realised how serious the position could be and had concealed some papers. Fortunately no one had, and the Japanese departed.

In our short time in this camp we had become aware of the sinister reputation of the Japanese camp commandant, Lieutenant Sonai. He was reputed to be as strong as a bull and his bashings were said to be fearful. So great was his reputation that when, on the following day, Sonai himself came to inspect us, we were at great pains to do nothing to rouse his anger. His inspection passed without any incident and after a quick look at our quarters, being apparently concerned with the condition of the sick, he strutted in front of us all as we stood to attention, and he proceeded to act as a doctor. Those whom he thought more sick than the others he ordered to the front and when he had finished about one-fifth of our number were ordered by Sonai himself to the camp hospital. When they left we were able to spread ourselves a little more, and so were more comfortable. The doctors had managed to obtain some medical supplies, and the worst of the men left were given injections and extra food.

I shall never forget Christmas Day of 1943. I shared my special food with two medical orderlies who had been very good to me at Haruku, and we had it in a small room used by the orderlies to dispense the medicines and dressings. The camp had put on a special meal on that day too, so we had a glorious "blow out". That Christmas of 1943 we relished the forgotten tastes of bully beef and condensed milk far more than I would relish any dinner that could be prepared for me now. But our poor, tired stomachs couldn't take such good, rich food, and I had violent diarrhoea for the next few days. Did I regret the food? Not in the least. It was a wonderful day.

We were given the name of the Queer People, and Haruku was known afterwards as the Queer Island for, although we didn't realise it then, we must all have been a little mad. In fact, it would have been remarkable if, after the long stay at Haruku and our 28 days in the ships, we had not been a little queer. I am afraid that some of our members disgusted a lot of those in Bicycle Camp who could not understand that food meant so much to us, and the food in Bicycle Camp was to us good. It was, in fact, as good as the food in almost any camp that I was in. We had rice for breakfast, and a loaf of camp-baked bread and soup for lunch, and at night a very good stew and rice.

The bread was not made from wheat flour, but a mixture of rice, tapioca and bean meal, which was called Asia flour. Loaves baked of this flour were usually doughy and of a different flavour from wheat bread. As each loaf was a fair size, about 6 inches by 2 inches by 2 inches, some of the POWs didn't use all theirs and the remains were thrown into the rubbish tins. It disgusted some of the comparatively well-fed people outside our area that, as the carts containing the rubbish cans came through our part, some of the boys raided the rubbish tins and retrieved this wasted bread, and any other edible things that were found. I didn't take part in these raids for I always had a good supply of food, but otherwise I would have been quick enough to join in. Later, I was to see these critics of our disgusting behaviour returning from raids of far more noisome rubbish heaps.

My greatest joy at this camp was the hot mineral water which we could use in abundance. At first we were confined to using the small tank of hot water and the few taps in our courtyard, but later, when we were out of quarantine, we were able to use the large tanks, or "tongs" as they were called. You didn't immerse your body in them but dipped water out with a bucket or any sort of ladle and poured it over yourself.

Continual washing of my clothes soon got rid of the lice in them, but unfortunately not all of the men cared about cleanliness and it was easy to become reinfected with these horrible vermin. Our scabies were treated with a mixture of sulphur and oil, and we were soon free of these nasty little insects that burrow beneath the skin and cause a horrible irritation. As we were sleeping on the tiles we kept bed bugs in check by putting our blankets in the hot sun.

During our stay in quarantine some of us used to wait at night until the guard was looking away and quickly nip out and into the main camp. Once there we were quite safe as long as there were no guards about. I had been told that a New Zealand pilot, Ernie Gartrell, ran the bakehouse, and it became a nightly venture to go to see Ernie. Usually I came back with my battledress full of loaves of bread, which I shared with some of the boys. Quite often, too, I was able to get some cucumbers, and I have vivid memories of sneaking back to bed and having a feast of fresh bread and cucumbers. Another New Zealand officer was in charge of making peanut butter for the camp, and I was fortunate in this bond too.

The activities of Bicycle Camp were startling to those of us who had come from Haruku. First, we realised that the camp ran a tobacco factory, for we were given an issue of cigarettes made there. Then we found that the camp had its own bakehouse, its own soap factory, and made peanut butter. What was even more amazing to me was that the camp made its own carbon paper for use in keeping records. False teeth were also made, but both the teeth and the plate were cast in aluminium. It was a startling sight when one of the boys laughed and exposed a mouth full of shiny aluminium. These were the activities that I came to know about, but I feel sure that there were many others.

The soda for the soap was obtained from the ashes of the cookhouse fires, and the work was all done by the prisoners, who received at this time ten cents for a private and fifteen cents for an NCO. At all times working parties were doing work outside the camp, and they received the same wage. The officers received a fixed sum each month according to their rank. We of Haruku did no work during this stay in Bicycle Camp.

Chapter 18

BATTLE OF SUNDA STRAIT

A fellow countryman I met in Bicycle Camp was John Thode, an officer of the Australian cruiser *Perth*. I had many good times sharing his bed space, drinking his coffee, and smoking his tobacco. From John I heard the tremendous story of the fight that *Perth* and *Houston* (an American cruiser) waged during the night they sailed into the midst of a huge Japanese naval force and a convoy it was protecting. This naval battle was truly an epic one, and because it is little known I shall give here an account of the story John Thode told me.

After the disastrous Battle of the Java Sea the light cruiser *Perth*, accompanied by the heavy cruiser, *Houston*, arrived at Batavia to refuel. Because the fate of a number of warships was not known and the amount of fuel was limited, they could receive only a small amount of fuel, but were ordered to sail to Tjilatjap on the south coast of Java and refuel there. At 1900 hours the two ships cleared the protective minefields, and set course for the Sunda Strait through which they would have to pass to get into the Indian Ocean. According to air reconnaissance the passage should have been clear of enemy shipping, and Captain Waller ordered *Perth* to be at second degree of readiness. At 2300 hours everything was quiet and the ships made their way through a calm sea in moonlight.

And now, because it is some years since John Thode told me the story in his own words at Bicycle Camp, I will quote from a report compiled by another officer of *Perth*, Lieutenant Commander J.A.Harper, R.N., and recorded by the Naval Board, Melbourne, in October, 1945.

> At 2306, when in position 5° 50'S, 106°10'E. (approx.) a vessel was sighted about 5 miles ahead, close to St. Nicholas Point. It was expected that she was one of our corvettes on patrol in Sunda Strait, but she was challenged by Aldis lamp as a matter of course. A strange reply on a greenish coloured lamp was made. The challenge was repeated, at which the vessel turned away and began to make smoke. When her full silhouette was presented to us it was seen that she was a Japanese destroyer. Captain Waller immediately ordered the alarm rattles to be sounded and the

forward turrets to open fire.

Course was altered immediately to bring the full broadside to bear. Shortly afterwards other destroyers were sighted to the northward and the armament split so as to engage more than one target at the same time. An enemy report of the first destroyer sighted was made immediately, and later, when an enemy cruiser was sighted, this was amplified to one cruiser. Captain Waller himself handled the ship throughout the action, altering course repeatedly so as to keep the armament bearing on the most suitable target or targets. *Houston* followed our motions throughout. During the action we actually steamed in a large circle, at one time being forced quite close in to the islands in Bantam Bay.

I cannot attempt to estimate what force was opposing us. During the action a large number of destroyers engaged us from all directions; at least one and probably more cruisers were engaging us from the northward and one officer on the bridge reported sighting a large number of vessels in close formation, probably transports. At about 2340 one set of torpedo tubes was fired from the bridge at a target — I do not know what. The other set was fired before the ship was abandoned, but I do not know if they were fired at a target or not. Due to a large number of enemy destroyers opposing us it was impossible to engage all targets at once and so some were eventually able to close to a very low range. By about 2350 one or two destroyers were close enough to illuminate us with their searchlights from a range of about 3000 yards.

Little damage was caused to *Perth* until the very end of the action. At about 2350 a shell entered the ordinary seamen's messdeck from the starboard side, forward, near the waterline. I also observed a small fire either near the catapult or in the after superstructure, evidently caused by a shell hit at about the same time. It was not until after the order to abandon ship had been given that many shell hits were received.

Damage inflicted on the enemy it is impossible to assess. Due to the extreme visibility and consequently the range at which most of the action was fought, it was difficult to observe the effect of the gunfire. Hits were definitely scored, both by the main and smaller armaments, on some of the destroyers which closed in.

A report on the action published in the *Japan Times Weekly* in about April 1942, indicated that we had caused quite considerable damage to the enemy, both warships and transports, and the transport carrying the general commanding the landing force appears to have been sunk.

At about midnight the Gunnery Officer reported to Captain Waller that very little 6 inch ammunition was left, so Captain Waller decided to attempt to force a passage through Sunda Strait. He ordered full speed and altered course direct for Toppers Island. We had barely steadied on the course when the ship was struck by a torpedo on the starboard side abreast the forward boiler-room or engine-room. The time would have been about 0005, the action having lasted just an hour. Captain Waller's

> remark was "That's torn it" and he ordered to prepare to abandon ship. A few moments later I drew his attention to a torpedo track approaching from the starboard bow, and this torpedo hit on the starboard side roughly abreast 'A' turret. Captain Waller then gave the order to abandon ship. The ship had already started to list to starboard and still had considerable way upon her. After an appreciable interval of five or maybe ten minutes a third torpedo struck well aft on the starboard side. This was followed shortly afterwards by a fourth torpedo, which hit on the port side; the ship then righted herself, heeled over to port and sank at about 0025. The ship's position then was approximately 5° 49'S, 106° 5'E. U.S.S. *Houston* was still fighting although badly on fire. She was hit by torpedoes and sank shortly afterwards rather closer inshore.
>
> Most people abandoned ship between the second and third torpedoes. I do not think that any boats were successfully launched, but I did observe that the 2nd cutter had been lowered; then Carley rafts and the wood merchant ships' life rafts were launched. While abandoning ship *Perth* was under fire and many hits were scored and casualties caused due to this. The pompom ready-use locker on the flagdeck was hit and exploded, killing several of the flagdeck and bridge personnel, who were descending from the bridge at the time. A hit was also received on the 4 inch gundeck. Many others were killed or wounded in the water by the explosion of the third and fourth torpedoes and by shells exploding in the water.
>
> The above report is compiled from a few brief notes made by me six months after the action and which I was able to retain throughout my imprisonment. Impressions of such an action are naturally very confused, and although I was able to discuss it with some officers and men during the ensuing five weeks, I was in no position then to commit any facts to paper. I was then separated from all but four other officers, and it was not until five months later that I was able to note down the few facts I could still remember.

In an article which was written by Commander Winslow, U.S.N., who was on *Houston*, and which was printed in the February 1949 issue of the *United States Naval Institute Proceedings* Winslow estimates the Japanese force as one of six cruisers, 20 destroyers, and 60 fully loaded transports.

John Thode managed, with others, to reach an island. After one of the ship's boats was washed ashore, he took command of a number of men and they sailed it through the Sunda Strait, eventually arriving at Tjilatjap, only to be taken prisoner. And so we met at Bicycle Camp.

Chapter 19

ADEK PRISON

Commandant Sonai, of Bicycle Camp, we regarded with a great deal of awe. When we first met him he had seemed quite normal; even slightly human when he picked out the sick to go to hospital. But we were still afraid of him. After the sick men he had himself selected had been in hospital about four days, Sonai paid a surprise visit to see how his patients were getting on. We who lived just the other side of the wire had our first indication of this when our siesta was broken by a roar as if some wild animal had gone mad. I must admit that most of us were afraid during the half-hour that followed. From the hospital next door came the sounds of furniture being smashed and thrown about. There were great crashes as many pieces of glass were broken, and throughout this time orderlies could be seen running and trying to get out unseen. We wondered what had gone wrong and whether we would be visited next.

After quiet had settled again we started to move around to find out what had happened. It was all to Sonai's credit. Perhaps when he paid his surprise visit Sonai had been told that all was not as it should have been at the hospital, and he had come to see for himself. He found that the boys from Haruku that he personally had picked out as being very sick were not in the hospital proper, but were out in the open porch with no comfort whatsoever, while in the beds and in small private rooms were installed Dutch doctors and orderlies. The sick he left alone but he wrecked the hospital furniture, beat up the orderlies and broke up their beds. In the kitchen where the hospital food was cooked he must have known that much was amiss, for he wrecked it so completely that it couldn't be used. He had one of the orderlies post a notice on the door saying that by order of Sonai it was closed.

Up until this time the hospital run by the Dutch had been a comfortable billet for a lot of Dutch orderlies and doctors and numerous other Dutch, who were in there for the comfort they received. From this time on the whole place changed. Our sick were moved into more comfortable quarters inside, and a great number of fit men were shunted out into the main camp. The food for the hospital was then drawn from the nearest of the three camp cookhouses, and our friends in hospital told us that this ration of food was half as much again as had been given from the hospital kitchen. What a racket had been going on! Our friends also told us that when Sonai threw out the kitchen table, attached to one of the legs was a dog.

My experience of Sonai was that he administered the camp well. Certainly he gave out some terrific bashings. When he started on anyone he seemed, as most Japs did, to go mad, and once started, he couldn't stop; but he enforced great discipline on his guards, and they feared him as much as we did. One good thing about Sonai was that he would not allow his guards to touch a prisoner. He insisted that if any beatings were to be done, he had to do them. Those he gave were hard, but in a camp of about five thousand one man could not beat a great percentage.

Of course I was only in Bicycle Camp for a very short time and I did not know the whole story. Sonai for quite a time was one of those who trained the young Indonesians who were brought into the Japanese army and called Hi Hos. Some of them acted as guards on working parties, and were very young and frightened. By talking to some of them I found out that they were chiefly conscripted into the Hi Hos. It is interesting to remember that the Hi Hos were later the main army of the Indonesians.

Unfortunately our stay at Bicycle Camp was not very long, and after a month or a little longer we were ordered to move. Early one morning we were paraded before the Japanese guard house and our kits were searched. Then, after a long wait, we were marched outside the camp and herded on to trucks. We were driven for a few miles at a frightening pace through the suburbs, and then into a prison-like structure surrounded by a high wall topped with jagged glass. The trucks stopped in an open space and we were ordered to the ground and counted again. Inside we found that our new home was really a prison, though the Dutch did not call it that. They called it some less forbidding name as it was previously used to hold coolie labourers who were being recruited to form large working parties for the plantations of Sumatra and elsewhere, where labour was in short supply. These poor, ignorant coolies would be induced to put their mark on a contract for an advance of money. Having made their mark they would be signed up to work for the Dutch for a period, which I believe was usually five years.

During the time of recruiting the requisite numbers — and this at times might take months — the coolies were locked up in large prisons such as our camp at Adek. They were allowed no contact with their relations and friends unless their wives were going with them, and then these were locked up, too. If they escaped or broke their contract they were treated as criminals. It was virtually slavery, but for many years it was the way the plantations were worked in areas where labour was not available. In Sumatra were extensive tobacco plantations where the finest leaf for wrapping the outside of cigars was grown. The Americans were the largest buyers of this tobacco and eventually, after repeated requests that the Dutch put a stop to this practice, they forced the issue by refusing to buy any more tobacco until something was done. The only change, however, was that a coolie who broke his contract was not charged in a criminal court, but in a civil one. Then it wasn't slavery.

When I was on my way to Singapore in the first place we sailed from Wellington in a small Dutch ship called *Tasman*. On our way to Sydney and during our stay there we were conscious of a very peculiar smell which pervaded the ship. It was not until we had left Sydney and were sailing up the Great Barrier Reef and the weather became very hot that we learned the reason for this smell. The hatches were taken off and to our amazement we found that we had a cargo of Javanese coolies housed between the decks. These coolies had been working in the sugar plantations in New Caledonia for the French and, though their contracts had not expired, the loss of France to the Nazis had made money short, and they were being sent home with no reward at all for their years of hard labour. Afterwards I often wondered if the presence of these coolies was known to the authorities in New Zealand, for the *Tasman* was at least six or seven days in Auckland Harbour and as long in Wellington.

New arrivals from Bicycle Camp were certainly qualified for residence in such a jail as this, for we by now were coolies of some standing. The Japanese had told us that this camp was to be a camp of relaxation and ease, and that in it we could get fit and well. Probably the higher officers had ordered that it should be so, but it turned out to be a very strict, disciplinary camp.

At Adek there was no Japanese officer in charge, and the guards could do as they liked. From the start they bullied us and imposed the strictest discipline that I experienced in any camp during my captivity. Here at Adek all commands were given in Japanese and we had parades on the slightest excuse. These had to be carried out with great precision and all clothing had to be as clean and as neat as possible. If a garment had buttons they had to be fastened correctly or there would be a bashing.

To make matters worse, we had no officer of our army to take charge of us. In fact the only officers in the camp were the two doctors. The NCO's had to run the camp. If the men had been fit it would not have been so bad, but the main crowd at Adek were the boys from Haruku who were still far from fit and not very keen on enforced discipline, particularly when it had to be enforced by an NCO, and when there was no higher authority to whom it was possible to appeal.

During all of my imprisonment so far I had been living amongst English soldiers, and I found myself accepted by them and quite popular. At Adek I was compelled — very reluctantly — to take charge of men. I had to be in charge of a room containing almost 100 men, all from Haruku and all more or less sick. If conditions at Adek had been the same as in other camps all would have been easy, but these boys hated the host of new restrictions that the Japs imposed, and of course they didn't co-operate very well. As a result of this we had frequent trouble with the Japanese guards, who beat up any culprit and almost always the "hancho" too, as the hut commander was called. In time I organised a disciplinary squad amongst our own hut members, and we administered our own punishments. Usually it was a ducking in a dirty pool or similar humiliation, but the grand thing was that it worked.

It is hard to describe the tension and fear that was about us all the time in Adek. Each day we had two parades for tenko. At these parades all commands had to be given in Japanese. The numbering had to be perfect, for the one that made a mistake would be beaten, and if the parade was slovenly or any fault could be found the hancho was beaten, and we would have to wait at attention for an hour or more.

The commands would be something like this: as the Jap approached to take the tenko I would shout "Kyotsky!" (Attention!); then as he drew near, "Kaishiri minge!" (Eyes right!), then "Nauri!" (Eyes front!), then "Bango!" (Number!). While I hoped fervently that the men would do it correctly the numbering would go on — ich (1), ni (2), san (3), she (4) etc. If the count was right the Jap would leave, and as he passed I would have to shout "Kaishiri idaria!" (Eyes left), and when he turned the corner to go to the next room I would give the order which was most delightful to all: "Yesame!" (Rest). The parade would not be dismissed, however, until all the rooms had been counted and then as the Japanese came past on his way back to the guard house I would have to shout "Kyotsky!", "Kaishiri idaria!", and after a pause, dismiss. The tenko Jap was almost invariably the same one each day, and he always carried a piece of bamboo with which to beat up anyone he thought at fault.

One of the duties which caused a great deal of trouble was that of fire watching. During all the hours of darkness one of the prisoners had to be on guard, and was supposed to parade up and down in front of our room. This duty was for hourly spells and was allocated to the men on a roster system. It was part of the duty of the fire guard, after he had done his term of an hour, to waken the next man and see that he went on duty. Time after time the chaps would fail to go on duty with the result that the Jap guard on his rounds would find no one on guard, and go mad. He would switch on all lights and bellow for the hancho. When I appeared he would always beat me about the face, and then the offending first guard would get a beating. Sometimes the whole room had to stand at attention for an hour as an extra punishment.

It was the constant failure of the fire guards to do this small duty that made us organise our own punishments. Certainly being fire guard was not a pleasant duty, for whilst on duty the guard had to be on the alert for any Jap who might be in the vicinity, to whom he would have to bow, or salute if he had on a hat, and say in Japanese that there was no fire, and that everything was in order. It was quite difficult to remember the correct Japanese words, and if they were wrong the Jap would often give the guard a beating. But this failing would not involve the whole room, as failure to be on duty did. I think the Japanese found pleasure in finding something amiss, for it enlivened their duty hours.

Except for myself the 120-odd men in my hut were English, and most of them conscripted Air Force lads. I found that the majority were extremely dirty, and careless about personal hygiene. Our room was a very crowded one, and we had to sleep man against man. I was fortunate to have clean chaps about me, but some were not so lucky and complained bitterly about the filth of their neighbours. I tried, by talking to the room, to get a little cooperation from the very dirty ones, but with no result. I saw the doctor and asked him to make a rule that all men must have a shave each day. This camp at Adek was well fitted out with bathing facilities, and I was having two or sometimes three showers a day, for it was our only pleasure. For me it was hard to understand that most of the men found it a burden to have one shower a day, and some just ignored the rules altogether.

Some of these men were so filthy and washed so seldom that they were infested with "crabs". The worst were so bad that they had them in their eyebrows. When some of the boys complained that in the morning they found crabs crawling on the tile floor I checked and found it to be correct. We took action and the squad forcibly gave these dirty ones baths. These baths were enforced by a gang of stronger English men, and were a great source of amusement to the room. In fact, our disciplinary measure raised the morale of the chaps tremendously. Games were allowed in the afternoon, and cricket and soccer were played, but not too strenuously.

The food in Adek was inferior to that of Bicycle Camp. It was rice pap for breakfast, bread and soup for lunch, rice and stew for dinner at night. As hancho I had to see that the food was distributed evenly. It was a very hard job, since cooked rice swelled to a different amount each day. The quantity of stew and soup also varied each day and so one had to be very careful to make sure that the measure decided upon for the issue would in fact go round the 100 men. Any left over was distributed on a further system. As each meal was being served, two or three scrutineers were always in attendance to make sure that no one received more than his fair share. I am afraid that there was very little give and take exhibited, and there was always someone who had a complaint. When, however, it was suggested that these dissatisfied ones be scrutineers they were not so keen: they were just too lazy. Later, I was to serve food for a similar number of Australians where the food and conditions were very much worse, and I had no trouble whatever.

During our stay in Adek we had one serious incident that will help to explain our fear of the Japs, and why we so often stood and allowed a Jap who was a lot smaller than ourselves to beat us up without trying to strike back. Since I have been home quite a lot of people have told me that their reaction to a beating would have been to hit back, implying that they thought we were poor fish not to do so. Earlier, I mentioned what would have happened, but I will relate this story to explain it now.

During the evening tenko an Australian who the Japs knew was going a little mad (they had been told so by our doctors), suddenly rushed up and struck a Jap. Immediately, a guard was called and the Aussie was beaten senseless and taken away. The room commander in charge of this Aussie received the same treatment. All the rest of the camp were kept standing at attention for almost three hours, and when dismissed were not allowed out of their rooms even though a meal was being served.

The doctors went out to try to help, and repeated that this Aussie was mad, but the Japs wouldn't listen and gave the doctors a beating, too. Later the two men who slept on each side of the Aussie were taken over to the guard house and beaten, and tortured all night by being made to kneel on concrete on which fine sharp gravel had been scattered.

After about three hours of standing at attention, when the tenko Japs re-appeared, our drill was executed perfectly and our numbering was wonderful to hear, for accompanying the tenko Jap was a large Jap carrying a great piece of wood.

When we were ordered to move from Adek after a spell of about two months, no one had any regrets. Actually many of us were a lot better in health. Although conditions were not good we had not had to work. And yet of our party from Haruku quite a number had survived the ordeals of the trip back to Java only to die in Bicycle Camp and Adek.

Chapter 20

BACK TO SINGAPORE

It was a refreshing change to be met at this new camp by the Australian CO, Wing Commander Ramsay Rae, and personally welcomed by him. It seemed to augur well for our stay there. Instead of the permanent buildings we had been used to in Bicycle Camp and in the prison at Adek, this place was a new camp and was made of long atap huts, some extending between rows of coconut palms. Something about the atmosphere of this camp seemed to affect us all and cheer us up. No one seemed to be grumbling as much as before and it was a pleasure to hear healthy, hearty laughter. The obvious fitness of the prisoners, too, was a joy to us. They played basketball strenuously. Australians were in the majority in this camp, and it seemed that they made the most of things. We found that not only the CO but all the rest of the Aussies welcomed us to this camp.

The work of the camp was in the gardens. We grew vegetables for ourselves and for the Japanese to market. A part of the gardens was right beside the camp, but the main area was about five miles distant, and we had to march to and from it each day. Reveille was about 3 a.m. and we had our breakfast as soon as we got up. Breakfast was a half-loaf of bread which was baked at Bicycle Camp and sent to us each day. With it we had tea and some jam that was made in the camp from pawpaws. At about 4 a.m. we had tenko and then we marched in the darkness to the gardens. There is something good about marching. Perhaps it is something to do with the rhythm, but at any rate I enjoyed these marches and so did most of us as we swung along the deserted road, singing. At the gardens we were issued with tools by the light of flares, and then we waited for the dawn before we started work.

The dawns in the tropics burst upon you. First there is the colouring from the sun's rays, and then the sun itself. Dawn here in Java, as with dawn in so many other places, marked the start of the working day. In a hot country dawn is even better than in more temperate zones, for then the air is cool and refreshing without a hint of the scorching heat which is to follow. I enjoyed these early mornings in the garden, sometimes hoeing, sometimes digging, and sometimes looking after the irrigation ditches which mean so much to crops in this area.

This last was the most enjoyable job in the garden, and when working at it I forgot all about being a prisoner for the first few hours. By nine o'clock the sun had taken charge, and it became a mental and physical struggle to complete any kind of work. Even though we did very little work at times we always had to be going through the motions of work, for the Japs had built high watch towers.

Some of the things I remember growing were cucumbers, pumpkins, marrows, sweet potatoes, tapioca and a lot of greens which took the place of spinach. These greens were creepers which grew very rapidly in the hot climate. I used to pick the green shoots and eat them raw if no one was looking.

About 10 a.m. we had a short break and were given tea and the other half of our morning loaf. Then we worked until about noon, and after handing back our tools we marched back to camp. This march was not nearly as cheerful as the one out, for everyone was exhausted by the hot sun. However, when we arrived back in camp about 2 p.m. we showered and rested, and were revived in time for dinner. This was the only camp where we got back from work at the time the Japanese had promised.

All too soon, we were told we were going back to Bicycle Camp. They said we would return in about ten days, but not many of us believed this, and we were downhearted at going away from this well-run camp. There were rumours that another working draft was being got ready to be sent overseas. This sent a chill into the hearts of many who had already been to Haruku on a working party, and some of them began making plans to avoid being sent. I hated leaving, particularly because it was the first camp that I had been in where there were more than a few New Zealanders. After work in the gardens I filled in my time carving tikis out of perspex.

Back in Bicycle Camp we found conditions generally the same, except that we had to start work each day between 7.30 and 8 a.m. Each morning we were paraded and counted, then required to scramble on to trucks for our hectic drive through the town to our place of work. The Japanese drivers seemed quite crazy, and drove at a mad pace through the crowded streets. Some of them were completely callous and purposely tried to run down the gharries (small horse-drawn vehicles which were used for carrying passengers round the city), to strike them glancing blows with the side of the trucks. At times as we approached a corner it seemed impossible that the truck could take it, but with tyres screaming, and us clinging on to each other and leaning into the corner the truck somehow managed to get around. In some ways I enjoyed the thrill of these drives as they put a little colour into the usually very dull day.

Most of the time we were digging air raid shelters in a large open park, which for some reason was called "Waterloo Plaster". In the hot sun this work was very trying and monotonous. We had a number of the Hi Hos as guards, but they were always closely watched by the Japanese. These young Indonesian recruits looked slightly bewildered and were afraid to talk to us. Occasionally, if we were well hidden from any chance of Jap observation, we could get a little information out of them. Most of them, they told us, had been forced to join, although it was claimed by the Japanese that it was an entirely voluntary movement. They told us that if a certain number of young men failed to volunteer from a native village the Japanese penalised the village in some way.

One day about twelve of us were taken to the "Kempei Tai" headquarters to clean up the gardens and paths. The Kempei Tai was the equivalent of the Nazi Gestapo. As the truck stopped immediately outside a window we were able to look inside. Around a table in the centre of a large, well-furnished room, sat three Japanese officers. They looked out at us for a few moments and I still have the memory of those sinister, intelligent faces. The other boys were affected in the same way. No wonder that the Kempei Tai put such fear into the Japanese troops and into the prisoners. Quite a number of our senior officers were taken in by the Kempei, and if they came back at all they returned as complete physical and mental wrecks.

Another job we had to do was build blast walls inside a large garage for motor vehicles. We built walls about 7 feet high and about 9 inches thick which I thought most foolish, for if a bomb landed beside them the bricks would make great shrapnel and add immensely to the damage. Still, I quite enjoyed the bricklaying; it was something new.

Our week at Bicycle Camp became a month, and there was no sign of going back to Makassura*. There were, however, persistent rumours of another sea voyage, and some of those who were trying to avoid the draft began to complain of complicated illnesses. Most of us were simply prepared to go where ordered. I was a confirmed fatalist by this time, and

---

Makassura was my third camp in Batavia. Situated just outside the city, we had gardens all around the camp and also we had to walk about 5 miles out from the camp to another large garden they had.

would do nothing to avoid any move. Though the thought of any episode such as Haruku was very disturbing, I made no plans to get sick.

As usual the rumours were correct and were eventually confirmed by orders to prepare for a move. There were always rumours before every move, and it would have been interesting to know where each one originated. Of course some were proved wrong, but so many were correct that we always thought of them as being potentially true.

The conditions at Bicycle were really very good, and though we would have gladly moved back to Makassura we would rather have stayed at Bicycle than move to an unknown destination. I found that we could do the work expected at Bicycle Camp on the food they gave us and still keep reasonably fit. In fact, though working, I was improving in health and fitness. Once again I must say that although the food here was very bad and the prisoners had a very just complaint, to us from Haruku it still seemed wonderfully good. Breakfast was tea and a loaf of bread, lunch (outside while working) was rice and soup, and for dinner a vegetable and meat stew and rice.

About two days after we had been told officially of our move, we were injected with some vaccine. A day later we were paraded early in the morning and then marched outside to the station to entrain for Tanjong Priok, the harbour of Batavia. Here the Japanese again went mad, and we were bustled on board a small ship in great confusion. I have no sure idea of the number of prisoners, but I would estimate that there must have been 500 of us who filled up the hold and crowded the deck. At night, after a very hot wait, we sailed. It was, of course, very well known to us all that allied subs were operating in the water we had to cross, but as there was nothing we could do about it we just had to try to forget that at any moment a torpedo might be rushing towards us.

During the night we were cold, but too soon after the day had dawned in a rush of glorious colour it became increasingly hot, and we were scorched. To most of the men the conditions on board this ship were terrible. To myself and the few other chaps who had come from Haruku, it was a pleasure cruise. A reasonable amount of food arrived from the Japs each day, and there was hot tea available most of the day. Our chief discomfort was the heat of the sun during the day and the cold in the night. There was no room to sleep lying down so we just dozed off where we sat. The trip was a short one and, as we had anticipated, our first stop was Singapore. We arrived in Keppel Harbour early in the morning after two days' and three nights' sailing. We were lucky, for the next draft to cross to Singapore — which included a lot of the chaps who by feigning sickness had avoided ours — were torpedoed and drowned. It was incidents such as these that strengthened our fatalism. It became part of our way of life never to try to organise things.

Chapter 21

SUMATRA JUNGLE

Our ship tied up at the wharf and we were disembarked, paraded with our gear, and counted. Then we were marched through part of Singapore to our new camp. I think we marched well, and I know that we sang at times. The English always seem to sing during times of adversity, and from our marching and singing the crowds of Chinese that lined the streets must have thought we were far from being downhearted. Surprisingly, Singapore did not look much different. The shops looked as if they were not doing their former roaring trade, but that was probably because of lack of goods. I noticed that the fruit stalls were well stocked. How we wished we could have raided them.

Our camp was an old one, formerly used by the Indian army. One innovation was that the camp guards were Sikhs, with Japanese supervising. I believe that the Sikhs were the only native troops to go over to the Japs, but they were lenient guards and did no beating up. They were chiefly concerned with seeing that no one escaped, and not with the discipline of the camp. The internal guards were Japanese and Korean.

At first sight River Valley Road Camp, as it was called, looked to be just a number of broken-down atap huts not fit to house anything. Most of the sides were gone and part of the roofs had been torn away. Quite a number of huts were partially collapsed, and some were totally so. These huts, when built, had two floors. The bottom part had an earth floor, and running the length of the hut on both sides were boarded platforms about 6 feet wide. A distance of 6–7 feet divided the two platforms. The top floor was similar, but with wider platforms and with ladders running up every 2–3 yards. The top floors were in the best condition, so we were housed in these. It was obviously a transit camp, and we wondered where we were going.

This camp was very extensive, and across a filthy canal which was one of the boundaries was another large area of atap huts in which other prisoners were housed. The Japanese prohibited our making contact with the men across the canal, and threatened to shoot any who tried. Some did try, of course. The first ones were a few sailors who came across from the other camp. I asked if any New Zealanders were among the crowd and they said yes, there was a chap named MacLeod among them.

The next day I went to the edge of the canal and, hidden by some pawpaw trees, spoke across the canal to some of the chaps who were washing at a tap. I asked if they would get Mac for me. Mac, when he appeared, was a tall, athletic type and we had quite a talk. I told him I would try to get across to see him that night. The sailors had waded across the canal, but it was such a revoltingly filthy place that I refused to consider getting across that way. I thought of sneaking across the bridge when the Jap guard was away for a few minutes. That night, accompanied by Ron Reid, one of the pilots I had rejoined at Makassura, just out of Batrama Camp, I crossed the bridge during a temporary absence of the guard and we had a great talk to MacLeod.

From him we learned the story of the men on his side of the canal. They had been taken prisoner in Sumatra after escaping from Singapore and had spent most of their time in a prison camp at Medan in northern Sumatra. They had broken camp and been loaded on to a ship which, accompanied by other ships and a Jap destroyer, set sail for Singapore. The crowded ship had been torpedoed and many men had been drowned. The survivors, after a gruelling time, had been brought to Singapore and were now recuperating in the camp. It was a most enjoyable evening. On our journey back to our quarters we were nearly caught for, thinking that all was clear, we started to cross a bridge when a Jap at the other end started to cross, too. Fortunately we heard his heavy boots and were able to draw back into the shadow of the huts. A few days after this we were allowed to visit between camps.

At River Valley Road Camp food was sufficient in quantity, but very poor in quality. We saw practically no meat and had very few greens. Most of the greens we had were useless as food. In fact, our best greens were the tops of sweet potatoes. The others were chiefly the tops of tapioca plants which were indigestible and horribly bitter. They contained a lot of poison and unless cooked for quite a time upset our stomachs. For protein we had small, dried salt fish, each one 2–3 inches long. We baked them crisp, and ate them whole.

We stayed in River Valley Road Camp about a month, and during this time worked at the wharves, loading and unloading ships. Whilst working we met men from other camps in Singapore whose appearance was at first quite strange, for their hair was cut in the normal style, instead of short as we were compelled to have ours. This rule of short hair had been forced on us in Java and it was a crime to have hair longer than a quarter of an inch. It was one of the Japs' sports if they saw anyone with long hair to give it a vicious tug, and sometimes it meant a bashing.

One day some of the prisoners were working on a wharf to which was moored a German submarine. One of the Japs started to beat up some of the prisoners just to show off in front of the Germans. The German sailors, however, were not amused, and one of them jumped ashore and beat up the Japs. I think that if our positions had been reversed we would have done the same.

When I had been in Singapore before my capture the heat and humidity were so oppressive that the smallest exertion made me sweat. Now, as a POW in the same climate, I found that, although hot and sticky, the climate wasn't nearly so oppressive. Probably with our poor food our own bodies were not generating so much heat.

In River Valley Road Camp we had electric light, and some of us made immersion heaters for heating water by suspending in our billies an element made of two pieces of metal insulated so that they were about an eighth of an inch apart. On one we connected the positive wire and on to the other the negative. Of course the billy and water became alive but no one got bad shocks. The voltage at Singapore was only 110, and we were on fairly well insulated flooring upstairs. One of the good features of this camp was the showers. They were right out in the open and were just a concrete floor with about twelve upright shower standards.

After about a month rumours again foretold a move, and railway work was mentioned. We had heard of the Burma–Siam railway, and wondered if that would be our destination. We hoped not, as the stories of the work on the railway were ghastly and grim. We heard that a life had been lost for every sleeper laid. This turned out to be the truth, when civilian deaths as well as those of POWs were included.

Our destination was not the Burma railway. In some ways it would have been better for us if it had, for the worst part of the work in that area was past. We had to go to Sumatra to build a railway there. Later we found that when we left Java we were on our way to Japan, but I think that the torpedoing of the ships coming from Medan upset the Japanese plans and our party was sent with the survivors of the Medan party to make up the numbers for the railway work.

The voyage to Sumatra was uneventful. We left in the morning, and on the following day, after sailing for hours up a large river lined on both sides with mud and mangroves, we arrived at Pekan Baru, a small town on about the same latitude as Singapore. Our vessel for the journey was a very shallow-draft ferry steamer and we felt reasonably safe, as torpedoes would have gone underneath if fired at us. Of course, we were crowded. We always were. But I have no memories of any special hardship, although I am sure it would make quite a good story if such a journey happened to anyone not conditioned to this sort of accommodation.

Our stay in Pekan Baru was very short indeed. We were hustled off the boat and marched to the rough new railway station buildings which were made of atap. Great piles of sleepers and rails were everywhere, and some POWs were working stacking rails when we came past them. At the primitive station we were ordered into trucks with metal sides and almost immediately set off towards the jungle that stretched away from the cleared area about the town. We were towed by large diesel trucks fitted with wheels to run on the railway tracks. Later we found that they could be quickly converted to run on roads too.

Our ride was a very bumpy one as the train swayed and bucked over the uneven track. It seemed to us that we would certainly be derailed. At a few places we saw gangs of POWs working, but the train didn't stop until we came to a large river with steep banks. Here we were ordered to walk across an unfinished bridge which spanned the river. The crossing was rather frightening as we had to step on the sleepers, which were loosely strewn across the main girders, and the drop to the river was very great. We were later to see great feats of engineering, for the Japanese constructed these long, high bridges with only the most primitive of equipment, and using material that was at hand in the forest.

After crossing the bridge we had a long, tiring march for about 5 miles in the darkness. All we could see at the end of it was the glow from cookhouse fires shining on the glistening bodies of the cooks as they did their work.

We were counted in the darkness, so this took a long while, but eventually we struggled into camp and were shown into atap huts which were to house us for we didn't know how long. These atap huts were crudely made with the usual 6 foot platform of rough, 9 inch by 1 inch boards along the length of each side and raised about 2 feet from the ground. The space between the platforms was just earth, and in some of the newer huts roots and trunks of small trees had still to be removed and the ground levelled off.

This was Camp 5, and it was situated amongst rubber trees; but we knew nothing of this until the next morning, for our great concern as soon as we had eaten a meagre meal of rice was to get our heads down and go to sleep. To negotiate the passage in the hut and avoid barking our shins was a great feat in the darkness. Our only light that first night was from a bonfire outside in the open space. The Japanese kept it burning all night because this was tiger country, and they were afraid of tigers. Some of the largest tigers in the world are in Sumatra.

Early next morning before it was light, we were roused by the camp bugler, and in the grey dawn we queued for breakfast. This was our first experience of "ongle-ongle", a grey-brown sticky mess that had little substance as a food but was chiefly water. It was made from the fine flour milled from the tapioca root. In Java there were two or three factories milling this tapioca flour. I had seen one of them when, before going to Singapore, I was a guest of the Anglo-Dutch Plantation Company. This tapioca flour was in the main exported to America as the base for fine glues such as stamp backing. Our breakfast was about a pint of this obnoxious stuff. It was about 90 per cent water and after about an hour we passed it all as urine. In Singapore we had been able to procure a little sugar, and for a few days we were able to use this to improve the vile taste of the ongle-ongle.

Our first day was filled with work inside the camp. We cleared up many of the stumps inside our huts and tried to get settled. For lunch we had about half a pint of dry rice and some boiled tapioca leaf. Dinner at night was about half a pint of rice and a few spoonfuls of stew, which was spiced and made quite tasty.

In the huts each man was allowed 1 metre (about 39 inches) as his share of the platform. This meant that he had a space of 6 feet by 39 inches on which to sleep, eat, etc. The latrines at Camp 5 were situated at the back of the camp and were large pits dug in the ground and covered with trunks of rubber trees. A series of holes were left which were covered, when not in use, by a wooden trap. At one end of the pit a fire was lit each day and its smoke helped to fumigate the rather smelly place. Compared to Haruku these latrines were quite luxurious.

Our wash place was some distance away, and to get there we had to bow and salute the Japanese guards as we went out the gate, walk along the road for about 400 yards and then enter the jungle swamp for about another 300 or 400 yards. Through the jungle we had to walk along the trunks of fallen giant trees, and our bathing place was composed of a mass of fallen timber from which we could scoop up water and splash it over our bodies. It would be hard to find a more difficult track or a more primitive washing place. Sometimes the monkeys came in droves to watch us bathe, and I am sure they ridiculed us in their own language.

Water for cooking came from wells we dug. We found the little Japs had a great fear of being taken by a tiger at night, and were reluctant to leave the fire that they always kept going in the guard house. For the first time we had no fence of any kind around the camp. The Japs knew that although anyone could easily escape he would never get far, for we were in a most desolate area composed chiefly of jungle swamps.

Chapter 22

CAMP 5 RAILWAY JOB

Some of the Medan boys were already in the camp when we arrived, and amongst them was my compatriot, Mac. From them we learned that the work was making the embankment for the railway line and that it was hard.

The idea of a railway through these jungle swamps was considered by people who knew the area to be fantastic — a job that would be almost impossible, even with the best of machinery. The Japs tackled it with practically no machinery. Their idea was to connect Pekan Baru with the railway at Padang so that trains could bring supplies to and from the nearest port to Singapore, which was Pekan Baru. The line was built in a south-westerly direction, and at one point crossed the equator. By the time we arrived it had been built as far as the bridge we had to walk over when we arrived in the darkness, but between this bridge and Camp 5 quite a lot of the embankment had still to be formed, and that was our first job.

All day we worked, from early morning to late afternoon. Some were digging pumice ballast from large quarries and loading small trucks which, when filled, were pushed by others along a light gauge track to the embankment, almost half a mile away. There the trucks were capsized, and another party of men spread the filling and formed the embankment. The work was very hard and the heat terrific, so that at the end of the day we were exhausted. Most of us worked stripped to the waist and our skin became very burned, but perhaps because of the great humidity we neither peeled nor blistered badly, and after a few days we were almost as brown as the natives. During the day we sweated continuously, and our shorts were permanently saturated. When we arrived back at camp we were counted very carefully, and then allowed inside.

Back at camp came the long task of having a wash. However tired I was I always thought it worthwhile, except when sick, to make the long journey to the wash place and have a refreshing bathe. Cold water on our tired bodies gave us quite a shock, but I had learned that cleanliness was a great booster of morale. Mac was another of those who always made the effort to have a bath, and during these expeditions through the jungle in the dark we formed a great friendship which lasts to this day.

In time our embankment work was finished and we started what was to be our main job — laying the rail tracks. First we spent days laying the sleepers and boring holes in them, so that the spikes that were to hold the lines on could be driven home easily. I was in camp with another of my regular doses of malaria and missed the first few days of rail-laying, but was told that conditions were chaotic, for the Japanese and the men were unused to the work, and the frequent hold-ups and mistakes caused the Japs to lose their heads completely. By the time I was over my bout of malaria the rail had been laid past the camp for a distance of about 10 kilometres.

When we paraded for work in the morning we were counted and then divided into smaller groups that were to do the different jobs, and issued with tools of different kinds. Then we scrambled on to the piles of rails that were stacked on bogies, which formed the train. The rails were approximately 30 feet long and were bolted on to a movable girder such as you see on timber trucks. This allowed the bogie to follow the curves of the track without the heavy load of rails doing the same. It was on this load of rails that we crowded and were towed behind one of the diesel trucks. Usually there would be about eight sets of bogies supporting four loads of rails. This journey up the line was a nightmare, as the rails would sometimes turn as the train jolted and swayed on the uneven tracks. Each small bridge was built higher than the rest of the track to allow for future ballasting, but the Japanese drivers never slackened speed and we careered along as if on a scenic railway at a fair. It still amazes me that we had no serious accidents, though the train was often derailed.

When we arrived at the end of the track we were again paraded and counted. Then work began with great shouting by the Japanese. First, the sleeper carriers pushed on further up the track to lay sleepers ahead of the rail-laying gang. Usually the sleeper carriers were about a day's work ahead of the rail-layers. They carried the sleepers from where they had been cut and stacked by natives. They were straight out of the jungle, and were green and very heavy.

Now for the rail-laying. Our task each day was to lay 2 kilometres of track. A kilometre is five-eighths of a mile, and even with the best of equipment this would have been a great task for one day. On the first day out from camp work started almost at once, but each day our travelling took longer, until sometimes it was almost noon before we started work. Regardless of the starting time 2 kilometres had to be done each day, so that the further we worked from camp the later we got back. Sometimes we didn't get home until midnight, but that was after we left Camp 5.

On my first day of rail-laying the train towed us almost to where the laid rail ended. Here the truck shunted the train on to a siding and then came around behind and pushed, so that the load of rails came right to the end of the track. The truck then went back for more rails, and work began. The rail-carriers were the first to move into action and eight men lined up on each side of the stack of rails. With a crisp "two-six-up!" the carriers on, say, the right side, would lift the dangerously heavy rails on to their shoulders, then all would walk in step between the end of the sleepers and the edge of the embankment until they came to where the right rail finished. There they would stay until a group of "lifters-off" took a firm grip of the rail at about arms' length. With another "two-six-off!" the carriers would slip from under the rail, the lifters-off would guide the rail as it crashed on to the sleepers and then move it so that it touched the end of the one laid previously.

As soon as the rail was down the spikers went into action and drove spikes into the sleepers to hold the rail firmly in place. The same sequence of work was going on at the same time on both sides of the line. The rails fell with a terrific crash alternately on the right and left, but never together.

Working in between the rails were the men jointing each length with fish-plates. On one side the spikers had also to carry a gauge, and the spikes had to be driven so that the gauge between the rails was always the same. After Camp 5 the sleepers, too, were brought loaded on top of the rails, and then the first to start work were the sleeper-carriers, who kept placing the sleepers only a few yards from where the rails were dropping. This simple explanation of the job as it was done does nothing to convey the great confusion and the danger in the doing of it, for the embankment had a width of only about a foot beyond each end of the sleepers, and in the length of only a few rails there toiled about 300 men — rail-carriers staggering under a weight they should not really carry but which they could not drop, because the falling rail could injure their comrades; spikers swinging heavy hammers and only stopping to let the rail go past; and sleeper-carriers, too, using their small area as they staggered under the weight of a heavy sleeper. It was one sleeper, one man. The fish-platers had, I think, the worst time, as they were cursed by everyone.

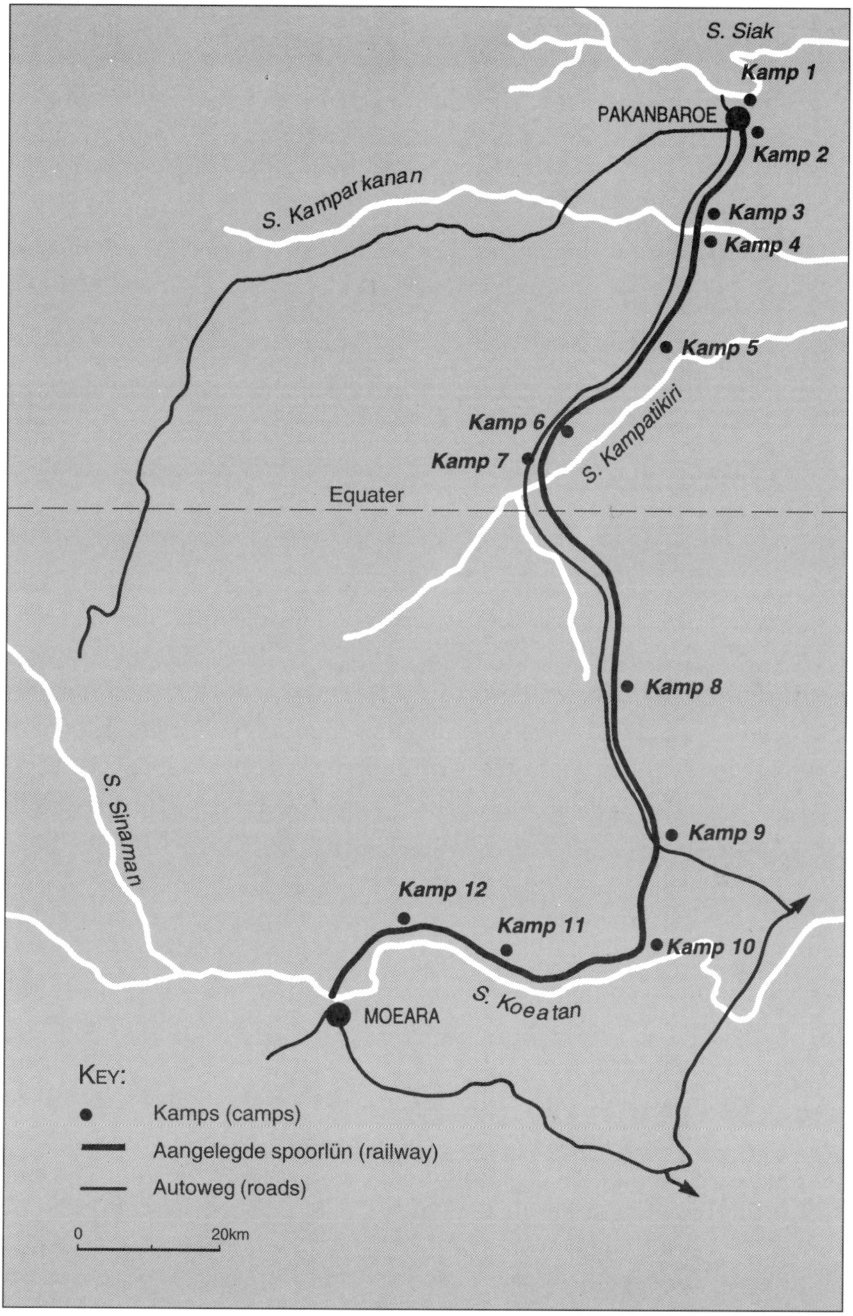

Map showing completed railway line from Pekanbaru (Pakanbaroe) to Moeara. The author worked on the line from Camp 5 to Camp 9. Work began from both ends of the line simultaneously.

They reminded me of scared rabbits as they scuttled in and out of falling rails and sleepers and swinging hammers.

The greatest menace to all to us was the Japs. Whenever we were laying rail they became demented with excitement, and screamed orders and abuse at us. Worse, they would beat up anyone handy if the work didn't go according to plan. I saw Japs throw hammers at men, kick them, and beat them with their rifles, because the job was held up for some unavoidable reason. I saw men struggling along with heavy sleepers on their shoulders pushed down the embankment for no reason at all. As each pair of bogies was unloaded they were pushed off the line and down the embankment to make room for the next load of rails to go past. At the end of each day they were put back on the tracks.

On my first day I was a rail-carrier. I found the work very hard, for a length of rail weighed about two-thirds of a ton and the usual carry was 60–100 feet. Each length was about 30 feet. If a rail fell it would surely have injured some of us, but the team spirit was good and this never happened during the time that I was carrying rails.

For a few days after this I worked as a lifter-off. This was easier in some ways, but not any more interesting. One day when working as a lifter-off the rail came crashing down on a small wooden bridge built across a tiny stream. These bridges had been built some months earlier, and a swarm of wasps had made their nest under this particular bridge. A length of rail was being carried to us when these wasps attacked us. There we were, standing naked except for a G-string, waiting for the rail while hordes of winged fury swarmed around us. They attacked the Japs near us too, which was a good thing, for these little warriors panicked and started waving their hats about their heads and this attracted the wasps to them. I was only stung in two places for I had been attacked by wasps before and had learned to keep still.

One day I was ordered by the Japanese to make up one of the spiking party. This job was dodged by the boys because if a spiker got behind with his work the Japs would always beat him up. I found that to drive a rail spike into the sleepers required quite a lot of skill. The heads of the hammers were long and tapered to the size of about a florin or approximately one and one-eighth inch at one end. The spikes we used had heads about three-quarters of an inch square. For a few days the Japs had men boring holes with augers but this took too long, so the boring was discontinued.

The spikes had a thread by which they should have been screwed into the sleepers, but they were old spikes being used a second time and they had been heated and a wedge point forged on them. We found that by driving the spike with the wedge in line with the grain of timber about half the sleepers would split. As long as the Japs were ignorant of this we kept splitting the sleepers; it was a mild form of sabotage, and also it made the spikes easy to drive.

I found the work of a spiker better than any of the other jobs, for it demanded a certain amount of skill. The better you became at spiking the less effort it took to drive a spike home. That meant a lot, for at spiking you only had a certain number to do on each rail and then you could wait quite safely till the next rail came down. Once we got used to spiking the Japs would not let us do other work. After a time it was amazing how easily we could drive home a spike, and I realised that by learning to use the minimum amount of effort I was saving myself valuable energy. I realised that this should make my chances of living greater. As the months passed and I saw the way the poor rail-carriers had to drain their strength, I felt more and more glad that I had mastered the art of spiking.

The work went on like this for month after month, and each day we completed our 2 kilometres of railway, whether it rained or not. Knock-off time depended solely on when we finished the 2 kilometres. Sometimes we were working 30 kilometres from the camp and then work would not be finished until sunset, and we had the long return journey through the darkness.

After our evening meal most of us would sit around the camp fire, and while some sang, others would be making a brew of tea or coffee. After a few nights a series of lectures were started, and Mac gave one about New Zealand. These sessions did not last for long, and before lights out sounded at 9 p.m. most of the boys were stretched out on their hard platforms asleep. The only lighting in the huts was a few flickering oil lamps. Each lamp was just a tin of coconut oil from which a wick drew oil up to the flame. Each night it seemed just a few minutes after going to sleep that reveille sounded and we had to start grimly on a new day.

Chapter 23

CAMP 6

Never will I forget the journeys back to camp. In Camps 5 and 6 we rode home by clinging to the frames of the chain of bogies, which after work were lifted back on to the line and coupled together. Each bogie was just a bare metal frame with four wheels and a swinging bar on the top on which the rails were carried out. We had to hold on like grim death to avoid being thrown off as the crazy Japs raced on the very uneven surface with the bogies swaying and bucking. If you slipped you would be caught amongst the uncovered wheels which often were turning between your legs. I have said that the Japs raced; I suppose their speed was not really great, but considering the state of the track it was a very dangerous and reckless pace.

It usually rained in the evening. If we had been having sufficient food and if our bodies had not been exhausted by the hard day's work in the boiling tropical sun, we would perhaps have found the rain refreshing, but in our condition it chilled us to the bone. Before we started home we were, of course, counted. When we arrived at the station we were counted again, and with us our tools, which I am sure the Japs considered far more valuable. If a tool was not accounted for we waited until it was found. Usually the trouble was the Japs' counting, but rarely was the tool-count over without quite a long wait. When the tools were found correct we were counted once again and marched outside the camp where our working party guards handed us over to the camp guards. Here we had another count before being let into camp.

A normal day comprised the following tenkos or counts:

(1) early morning tenko in the dawn after we had taken our food

(2) working party tenko inside the camp

(3) tenko as the camp guards handed us over to the working party guards

(4) division into parties and issuing with tools when each section was counted

(5) tenko after the trip to the job

(6) tenko after our half-hour lunch break
(7) tenko when work was finished
(8) tenko of tools back at station
(9) tenko by working party Japs
(10) tenko by camp guards before being allowed into camp.

After we had laid the track we started ballasting the line. To do this we had to lift the line and fill in under the sleepers with pumice, or with any soil available. The soil was dug by a gang of chaps with spades and loaded into small bamboo baskets, which were carried by other prisoners to the line and emptied beneath the rail. Then other prisoners with great wooden hammers drove the earth hard underneath each sleeper.

All the railway work was bad, being done under the boiling sun, but the hammering job was the worst. When we were ballasting there was no set amount of work to be done. Almost invariably we worked from dawn to dark, and during this long time the hammers, with only short breaks, lifted and dropped all day to a chant of "one, two, down!", "one, two, down!". The Japanese got used to the English words and when the tempo slackened they would scream the chant at a great speed. Although the work of laying the rail was harder and more dangerous, it was the ballasting we hated most. Most of us developed a sixth sense and were always conscious of whether a Jap was looking our way or not. If the Jap was not looking we stopped, but the moment he turned round we were working. If you failed to relax at every possible opportunity, your chances of survival were lessened. That was life on the rail job — a continual fight to conserve your energy.

We stayed in Camp 5 for about three months and worked every day. The only excuse to get off work was sickness, and it had to be serious to count. As the days went by the fitness of the men began to deteriorate slowly. We were in a bad zone for mosquitoes, and soon there were many cases of malaria. Then the supply of quinine tablets ran out and all the Japs would give us was the crude bark of the cinchona tree from which quinine is refined. We had to pound it into a kind of sawdust and eat large quantities of it. It was unbelievably vile stuff, containing many impurities and poisons, and as a cure for malaria was often worse than the disease. Later it was mixed with ongle-ongle and made into balls about the size of a large marble. The full dose for a day was thirty-six of these pellets.

Tropical ulcers also began to spread. These are terrible things that always go with slave labour conditions in the tropics. On the Burma–Siam railway job tropical ulcers were one of the greatest causes of death.

The most devastating combination on our job was dysentery and beriberi. Gradually we all suffered with beriberi. In fact, considering our diet and working conditions it is surprising that this alone didn't wipe out the whole camp. When dysentery struck down a prisoner it was quite often his death warrant. During the days of dysentery the body got no nourishment at all and the beriberi increased in an alarming manner. Soon the only men in the camp who were fit were the cooks, and they were usually Dutch.

Freud said that sex is the dominant thing in our lives at all times. I think he would have found this to be disproved had he had dysentery and beriberi with us in Sumatra.

After Camp 5 we moved to the end of the rail at Camp 6. Our previous camp had been surrounded by dense jungle and we always had a feeling of confinement. This new camp was built in waste pumice land covered with small scrub. The huts were the usual atap ones, and our sleeping space the same as before. One of the improvements was a good bathing place in the camp itself, and this made a great difference. In Camp 6 Mac and I formed a "consay" — a Chinese word for company. We shared everything, even to an extra spoonful of rice. If I was sick in camp but was able to get about I did my best to make some coffee or tea and have it ready when Mac came shivering into camp, and when the positions were reversed he did the same for me. I can still remember the joy of a hot cup of coffee or tea as I came back exhausted. I am sure that had it not been for our partnership neither Mac nor I would have come out alive.

Mac and I decided that as our clothes would soon wear out we would sell them to the natives and spend the money on food. As there was a blockade of this area the natives could not get any goods, and clothes were in great demand. We made G-strings of sacking to replace our shorts. It was, of course, considered a great crime by the Japs to sell clothing and it had to be done very secretly while on the working parties. Mac was good at this as he had been an inspector of schools in Malaya and could speak Malay perfectly. Gradually all our clothes went and we spent the proceeds on food. A lot of the chaps bought sugar, but we decided that as sugar was a carbohydrate and our diet was predominantly starch, sugar was a bad thing to buy.

We spent our money on chillies and tressie (the fish paste I described earlier). From the chillies we reckoned on getting a lot of vitamins, and the tressie was protein. I remember having a great feast on the anniversary of Mac's wife's birthday, for we sold my greatest possession, my battle-dress jacket. On special occasions we bought a little sugar to sweeten our coffee, but salt was what our bodies needed far more than sugar. The constant sweating exhausted our bodies, and the salt added to our food wasn't nearly enough. Lack of salt caused us to have bad bouts of cramp. If we had no salt of our own we had to parade sick and were given some. In about half an hour the cramp would be gone.

There was a great scarcity of cloth for bandaging wounds and sores. If you went to the sick bay to receive treatment ointment was applied, and you were given a piece of cloth just large enough to cover the wound or sore. You then went to the nearest rubber tree, which in Camp 6 was quite a distance, and made a gash in the bark. Then you could smear the latex on the edges of the wound and on the piece of cloth and stick the patch on as you would patch a punctured tube.

We made blankets of sacking, and from then on until we were released we were clothed in sacking. Later on sacks were greatly sought after, and their price was 20 guilders or roughly £3.

At dawn and in the evening the chattering of the monkeys in the distance seemed to us just like the cries of school children at play. These monkeys took a delight in watching us at work. Judy, a dog POW who lived with us in this camp, strongly objected to them, and would bark and become greatly agitated. The monkeys seemed to take exception to this, and would become very cross and shriek what I am sure was horrible language at her. Between the monkeys and the barking there was a terrific din.

Judy was one of the most interesting POWs. I met her in Camp 5. She was a well-bred pointer dog, a faithful and intelligent animal, and was honoured after the war with the Dicken Medal, the animal's VC. Her history was an exciting and interesting one. She was the official mascot of a small gunboat, HMS *Grasshopper*, which at about the time of the invasion of Malaya called at Singapore. Some of her crew were transferred to HMS *Prince of Wales*, and when this great ship was sunk, Judy was one of the survivors. After a short time she rejoined *Grasshopper*.

On a black Friday, 13 February, 1942, *Grasshopper* was bombed and set on fire. She was beached on an uninhabited island in the Rhio Archipelago and all the crew got ashore, but in the confusion Judy was left behind. When she was missed one of the sailors swam out and freed her from the chart room in which she was trapped. No water could be found on the island until Judy managed to find a spring below high-tide mark and led the men to it. They were taken from the island to Sumatra, and camped at Padang. When the Japs occupied Padang, these men, with other Allied servicemen, were taken prisoner. Judy was allowed to stay with them.

Shortly before Christmas 1942 the camp was ordered to Medan in the north of Sumatra. The men asked to take Judy but were refused, so in the few days before the departure they trained Judy to lie quietly in a sack, and when they departed she was successfully smuggled on to one of the trucks and so made the journey to the new camp. For a time Judy was kept out of sight, but eventually she was seen by the Japs. They said she must be shot, but fortunately nothing was done about it.

In June 1943 a new camp commandant was sent to Medan. He was Colonel Banno who had fought with the Allies in the First World War. The men spoke of him as being a kindly man, but his guard commander was a brutal, sadistic type. One day he was going to bayonet Judy but Banno stopped him and beat him up. Seeing that the commandant was on the dog's side some of the POWs approached him and asked that Judy be given food as she was an official mascot of a naval ship. He agreed, and Judy became an official POW and entitled to a ration. Medan under Banno must have been a very good camp.

But then came orders to prepare for a new move by sea. Judy was trained again to lie quiet in a suitcase. Again she was successfully smuggled on board the crowded ship. The ship was torpedoed and hundreds of POWs drowned but along with the survivors Judy was taken to Singapore where Banno was at the docks to meet them. Again the Jap guards were going to destroy Judy, and again on Banno's order she was spared.

After a short time in Singapore Judy and her fellow POWs were sent to Sumatra, getting there just before we did; they were established at Camp 5 when we arrived there. I came to know Judy well on the railway job. She hated Japs, and we were always warned of their approach by her low growls. She hated monkeys too, but at them she barked loudly and savagely.

Chapter 24

TAKE A TENDER RAT

On mornings after rain we found all manner of marks of wild animals, but saw very few of them. Sometimes the marks of tigers were quite clear and it was in Camp 6 that the Japs' pet pig, which was being fattened for a feast, was carried off by a tiger. Sometimes when we went to work up the line we found that a herd of wild elephants had camped the night on the embankment. They did a lot of damage, leaving great footprints about 18 inches across in the newly formed earthwork. One evening we finished laying rail beside an abandoned hut. It was in good repair when we left it but by morning it was strewn over about an acre of ground, and our embankment was badly knocked about. There were wild pigs about too, as one incident showed. A body or bodies were waiting one night in the morgue, and wild pigs broke in and ate some parts of them.

One animal we saw a lot of was a small squirrel, or tree rat. Its quickness was amazing. One moment it would be at the bottom of the tree and the next at the top. Often we passed fresh spoor of a herd of wild pigs and our officers asked the Japs to try to kill some for food, but they refused. Occasionally a Jap was talked into killing a monkey but these occasions were rare, and Japs were very poor shots. To us a piece of monkey was luxury.

All meat was a luxury. One evening after getting home from work earlier than usual we were waiting for our meal when a thin ginger cat came into the hut. Some of the boys petted it and fondled it, but when an Englishman called Porky, who was a butcher, was seen eyeing it with a certain grim speculation, the kinder boys took the cat outside and told it to be off for its very life. Fortunately for us the cat strayed back and as (for some reason I have forgotten) Porky was under an obligation to Mac and myself, we had first a share in the cat soup and then a portion of boiled cat. I must confess that I tasted it gingerly but I found it delicious and had far too little.

Other strange things we ate if we were lucky enough to get them were

"Hey — there's seven maggots in my rice!"
"You're lucky — the ration's only four!"

rats, huhu grubs, locusts, snake, iguana, crocodile, dog. In fact, almost any living thing that we could find we ate. To prepare roast rat we removed skin, gut, tail, head and legs, and grilled it skewered on a piece of wire. Huhu grubs and locusts were also skewered on wire to grill. To make a bracken-top stew we boiled the curled tips of bracken in water, added salt if we had any, and tressie also if available. The result was a horribly bitter brew that took a lot of getting down even when we were most hungry. The reddish bronze leaves of ferns similar to those that grow in ditches in New Zealand were a lot more palatable than bracken and we ate them if we found them, raw or cooked.

The nuts from the rubber trees, if baked almost to charcoal, were edible but if not cooked until burnt were poisonous. Quite a few men died from eating rubber nuts that were insufficiently cooked. We also ate some gaudy multi-coloured toadstools which we found in the jungle. They looked horribly poisonous but some of the natives ate them first and we were soon following their example.

In Singapore, I read in an Air Force Manual on forced landing in the jungle that the only things to fear were hornets, malarial mosquitoes, scorpions and leeches. The danger from wild animals was completely discounted. In Sumatra we found this to be true. We saw many snakes, but they always saw us first, and were off in a flash. Scorpions we treated with respect for their sting is very painful, but although quite a number of men were bitten none died from these bites.

Leeches were likely to be anywhere in the jungle and in the streams. When we had our half-hour break for lunch we would usually seek out some shade, and it became a habit to look carefully at the ground before we sat on it. Sometimes an army of leeches would be coming towards us from all directions. They were not much thicker than a darning needle, about one and a half inches long, and jet black in colour. If one of these fastened on to you it caused no pain and often it was not until the leech was a revolting bloated mass about a quarter of an inch thick that you felt it hanging from your skin. We found that a burning cigarette tip applied to the stern of a leech made it let go and fall off. If you pulled them off the head usually remained and was the start of an ulcer. I loathed these leeches. When a leech is sucking blood it must secrete some substance to prevent blood from congealing, and for hours afterwards blood would slowly ooze from the place where a leech had had its meal. Coming back to camp from an area infested with leeches, a working party sometimes looked like men returning from a bloody war. The water leeches attacked us while we bathed, and were larger and even more loathsome than the regular kind.

The insect I feared most, however, was the hornet. The Air Force Manual on dangers of the jungle had stressed the need to beware of making camp near a hornets' nest, for three stings could be fatal. The motto on the 100 Squadron crest was "Serang te Buin Janga Di Jolik" — "Don't poke a hornets' nest". This had made me a little apprehensive about hornets, and when I did get bitten I found that this fear was justified.

Out from Camp 6 the rail passed through a patch of rubber. Some of the boys had found amongst the trees a few of the earthenware cups that are used to collect the latex from the trees, and as they were useful articles I sneaked off work one day to look for one. All I found was an enraged hornet. I was stung only once, but it brought on a very nasty fever. It also brought me quickly back on the job.

While at Camp 6 we experienced some of the most violent electrical storms I have ever been through. We returned home from work during one of these. It was well after dark, and we were walking back along the track after ballasting near the camp. The lightning was attracted to the rails, and time after time it would strike them and then a ball of light would go racing along the lines. We kept well away from the steel. This same evening as we lined up for tenko before going into camp a terrific shaft of lightning struck a pile of rails, only about 12 feet in front of us. No one was hurt, but the front rank of the parade collapsed in a heap. On other nights sheet lightning played almost continuously and lit up the camp like daylight. It was a wonderful sight and went on for hours at a time. There was not much thunder with this lightning.

But the beauty of this and many other wonderful things in the jungle wasn't easy to appreciate. Our only real concern was getting extra food, for we were hungry every hour of the day. At any time after our largest meal, the evening one, we could have sat down and eaten a full three-course meal.

The greatest relief for this hunger was smoking. In all the camps smoking was my greatest pleasure and many times I was given a clout by the Japanese for stopping work for a moment to pounce on a butt they had thrown away. At first our doctors advised us not to waste our money on tobacco but to spend it on food. However they soon recognised the value of tobacco and did all they could to make sure that a supply was available. The quality was extremely poor and the price exorbitantly high, but it was more welcome than anything else except food. At times when the supply in the camp had been exhausted for a few days the tempers of the men became vile. Early morning quarrels were frequent and the language shocking even to us. The change in tempers after an issue of tobacco was like a miracle. With an hour or so of smoking in the evenings, the mornings became quite normal.

We smoked under difficulties, for we had practically no paper in which to roll cigarettes. Some of the chaps made pipes that were wonderfully good considering the primitive tools and materials available. Bible paper was our best cigarette wrapping. A mixture of old butts in a single smoke gave us as heady a feeling as whisky would have done had we been fit. In our abnormal mental state we planned quite seriously to spend no money on tobacco if we ever got home. We would, we believed, collect plenty for our needs on visits to theatre lobbies and such places.

Strong black coffee, too, gave us a great uplift. When we were in funds we would buy the coffee beans and, after roasting them, grind them up in an earthenware latex cup, using a fish-plate bolt as a pestle. I think the coffee we had then was as fine as any since. We took great pains in brewing it, and allowed it to simmer but never boil. We added a pinch of salt if we had any.

Chapter 25

CAMPS 7 and 8

In time we pushed our railway forward about 30 kilometres and after what seemed endless days of ballasting we moved camp to a site on a bend of a large river. Once again all the buildings were atap, but the camp was not built on a flat area. It was on a slope, and the huts were therefore on different levels. The jungle crowded in from three sides, and on the other was the river. Our washing place was not, however, in the river, but in a small creek in the jungle. It had to be approached by a very muddy, slippery path down a steep incline. It was very shallow and slow running and was full of water leeches.

The building of the line from Camp 7 met with one great hold-up. About 2 miles from camp the line ran through a long, deep cutting. The sides of this cutting were too steep, and were continually slipping. Because of this we were held up getting to and from work, and for many days we got back to camp after 11 p.m. By the time we had queued up for our meal and eaten it very little of the night remained for sleep because reveille was at 4.30 a.m.

I was sick in this camp. I had malaria in all the camps, but in Camp 7 I had additional trouble from kidney stones. There was no medicine to alleviate the pain. All I could get was extra tea. Doctors have told me since that the pain from this trouble is about the worst you can experience. I thought so then, myself.

Christmas Day 1944 was celebrated in Camp 7, and it was the only day we had off work between the start at Camp 5 and the end of the war. For quite a few days before Christmas our ration of food was slightly less and we understood that it was being saved for a special meal on our holiday. When the day arrived we were disappointed with the food and there were many complaints. The cause of the poor meal was a quarrel amongst the cooks, and though we had extra rice and a fair amount of stew it was shockingly cooked and almost ruined. However, Mac and I were entertained by some Ambonese, who turned on a great meal for us.

Part of our feast was nasi kuning, rice coloured a bright yellow with

"DREAMIN' OH MY DARLIN' LUV OF THEE"
AN ODD ODE TO A STEAK AND KIDNEY PIE — After Cyril Fletcher
COMPOSED IN A JAPANESE P.O.W. CAMP — JAVA
DREAMIN' OF THEE —
— DREAMIN' OF THEE —
— DREAMIN' ALL NIGHT LONG I BE —
— I DREAM OF THEE AGAIN, IN SUNSHINE —
— AND IN RAIN —
POP
— ALAS! — I DREAM IN VAIN —
— THERE'S ONLY RICE AGAIN!

saffron, the yellow colouring of curry, and a sweet dish called kolock. Kolock was made from pumpkin. The flesh of the pumpkin was boiled in water till it was pulp. Then into it was stirred quite a number of cakes of gula Java (a native sugar that tastes like fudge) and just before serving a quantity of santan (coconut cream) was stirred in. It was flavoured with cloves and a little ginger, and was delicious.

Santan, which is an ingredient in so many tropical dishes, is the cream that is made from ripe coconuts. It is one of the best foods of the tropics. It is made by grating the flesh of ripe coconuts and then pouring a little boiling water on the gratings, squeezing it with great pressure in a cloth. The cream that oozes out looks like dairy cream, but has a very different flavour.

From the time I was taken prisoner, I had tried to learn Malay. I would practise the language by talking to some of the Dutch native troops who were with us. By doing this I formed some great friendships with the Ambonese and Monardonese. They were wonderfully kind-hearted, and often if they had managed to get extra food would share it with me. One of them was a fine old chap called Papalayer. He came from Saparua, the island next to Haruku. The Monardonese were from the north of Celebes, and one of them was for a long time my spiking partner.

It was in Camp 7 that we were allowed to write a lettercard home. We were given the choice of about five messages we could send. The one I chose included the phrase "conditions not so hot". The Japs would never have allowed it to be sent if they had understood English idiom. Camp 7 was a bad camp in every way and we were glad that our stay was short.

Camp 8 was beside quite the largest station, apart from Pekan Baru, that we had seen on the line. There were no rushing trains and large buildings — only a few small atap huts — but it was a junction and had quite a lot of sidings. Not long after we arrived in Camp 8 the first steam train made the trip, and brought in a load of rails.

When the trains started coming up to Camp 8, parties of about 20 men would be called out at all hours of the night to fill their engines with water. The engine was run to where the line crossed a small stream, and we would form a bucket chain and for about an hour and a half poured water into the engine. It was most monotonous work, and since the men on these parties were not excused work next day, they had very little sleep.

The camp was built in a rubber plantation, and for the first time the Aussies were in a hut together. Mac and Ron Reid and I were included with the Aussies. It was a great improvement for us. The Aussies, under adverse conditions such as we had in these camps, were tops. Before captivity I had liked them quite well, but here their spirit was wonderfully good and there wasn't nearly so much discontent and moaning. The issue of food was done without the quarrelling that often happened amongst the English soldiers. For quite a while I was in charge of the Aussie hut, but this duty was simple compared to my experience at Adek and I enjoyed it.

THE ARMED MITE OF NIPPON!

The bathing facilities were not good, though better than at our last camp. There was a small bathing place inside the camp but it was chiefly used by people who were sick and remained in camp. The main washing place was beside the railway line just outside the camp. Sometimes if there was a delay we had our shower while waiting for tenko. We got quite used to bathing naked in front of the natives. It seemed to be quite a show to them, and we usually had an audience.

Our huts seemed to be smaller, and I think they had been built from materials that had formed Camp 6. In any case our sleeping space was reduced from the usual 39 inches to about 27 inches and this made life very crowded. In most camps the guards lived outside the camp, but here they lived inside, so we used to see them doing their PT. In their badly fitting uniforms the Jap troops generally looked very poor specimens physically, but when we saw them stripped we found that they were very well developed and they looked wonderfully fit. They had long bodies and short sturdy legs.

As all of our clothes had been sold by this time we were very short of money. The rates of pay had been increased a month or so before to 15 cents for privates and twenty-five cents for NCOs. The camp fund took 40 per cent of that. Inflation had set in very badly and an egg was five or six guilders (about £1) or nearly 50 days' pay. Some of the Dutch fared well as they still had a great deal of money. Sometimes they even had chicken which cost about £10. I had not seen an egg for years, until one day I found one in the dust. It was one of the highlights of my whole prison life. The egg was boiled and was lying on the dusty ground outside the Jap quarters. It had been opened and a spoonful taken out but I pounced on it and after sterilising it over the fire had it with my lunch. I was sick in camp at the time.

To make a little money I pinched some copper wire and a small punch from the garage part of the station and began making copper needles (these were sacking needles, sacking being the only material we could use to make clothes). I sharpened them with a piece of file which was already one of my possessions. Mac and I went into partnership over this and for each needle we charged two guilders. It was Mac's job to act as salesman. His main customers were the Dutch.

One day I took the punch back to the station, and, while the Japs had their lunch, tried to sharpen it. A Jap corporal found me doing this and I had a most terrible beating. My greatest concern during this bashing was not to fall down. If I had done so I would have been kicked insensible.

My face and shins were in a horrible mess when he had finished but after a few days I was right again. One of my cobbers saw the punch in the workshop later in the day and retrieved it for me.

One afternoon when the Japanese officer was away some of the guards got drunk on rice wine. One of them went berserk and just about wrecked the guards' hut. For a long time there were great crashing noises as he smashed the Japs' valuable crockery, and then he emerged from the hut and chased anyone he could see. We all kept inside the huts to keep out of his way. The other guards tried to stop him, but he would not be pacified. Later in the afternoon the Japanese officer returned and went to stop the commotion. Usually an officer even miles away would have been enough to subdue any guard, but this one was too drunk to care and he struck the officer. There was a great uproar until the guard was overpowered and tied up. Next morning I saw him before he was marched away and he had the fear of death in his eyes. He was executed that day.

All this time the health of the men had been growing worse and the very sick ones were sent back to Base Camp. It was harder and harder for our MOs to find men fit enough to go to work. This led to great trouble from the Japanese, and culminated in the doctors refusing to send more sick men to work all day in the heat. The Japs made dire threats to the doctors, but when these had no effect they took it upon themselves to say which of the sick should work. They had a parade of all men sick in quarters and from these they picked enough men to complete the working party of about 500 required each day while we were laying rail.

Of course the Japs had no knowledge of the sickness of the men, and some very ill ones who were sent out died. About this time one or two of our chaps were drowned in latrines. They were so enfeebled that they fell in and could not crawl out or attract attention to themselves.

The further we moved up the line the worse became our rations, although the rations of the men at Base Camp were roughly the same all the time. At every stop along the line the rations would be stolen until we at the end who were doing the greatest amount of work received the smallest amount of food. Our meat ration, too, had decreased, but I don't think that any of it was stolen. It was much too high, and at Camp 8, was only offal from the Jap slaughterings. By the time it had travelled up the line you could smell it a mile away.

Before Camp 8 our ration was about half a buffalo for the whole camp for about a week. This had to be divided amongst about 1000 men and was rationed out for about four or five days to be used as flavouring to the sambal; our ration of sambal was usually about two level dessertspoons. It was so tasty however, that even a spoonful would flavour our dry rice. Our greens came up by train, too, but they were practically always just tapioca tops. Tapioca leaf is similar in shape to a lupin leaf, but is larger and not so soft.

None of the offal sent to Camp 8 was wasted. The hide was singed to remove the hair and then cut into small pieces and cooked for hours until it became a jelly. The bones were broken and cooked and cooked until all goodness was taken out of them; even then they were taken out by the boys and chewed. Only the horns were left. At times the camp fund bought a water buffalo and we had extra rations. Lunch was worse at Camp 8 than before. Instead of dry rice we had a glutinous mixture of rice and tapioca.

The Japanese were concerned at the number of men sick in the camp instead of working, and issued an order laying down a different scale of evening rations for the sick and for the workers. In most of the huts the order was carried out, but in the Aussie hut sick men and workers received the same amount. Later it was amended slightly and the workers who needed more carbohydrates were given a little extra rice, but the quantities of the nourishing part of the meal remained the same.

By this time almost all of us had beriberi, but not too severely. We were getting worse, but it was a gradual deterioration if you did nothing to destroy the food balance between vitamins and protein and carbohydrates. But if extra carbohydrates in the form of tapioca, polished rice or sugar were eaten the balance was destroyed and almost overnight beriberi increased. To do this was almost like committing suicide. Hunger drove many to it, and then swelling progressed rapidly and often in a few days they would be in hospital. Sometimes the hospital diet saved them but often it was too late.

We had two forms of beriberi which we called wet and dry. The dry usually followed recovery from a bad bout of the wet and took the form of paralysis of the limbs and blindness. Some became deaf, dumb and blind. The wet beriberi was most common and caused a breakdown of the elimination of water from the body. This fluid gradually built up in the body until in the severe cases faces were like round moons with eyes that could hardly be opened. The stomach swelled and testicles became greatly enlarged.

I saw doctors many times perform operations to remove the liquid from a patient's stomach. Always about a four-gallon tin of fluid was taken away. This operation was performed on a table in the open. About four orderlies held the man down and the incision was made without any anaesthetic. It was only done as a last resort and was usually unsuccessful. If the Japs had given us a little extra good food they could have prevented this horrible malnutrition disease.

In Camp 8 some dudek — the coarse polishings of rice — was made available. A lot of the chaps either disliked its coarse, bitter flavour or did not realise its worth, and Mac and I were able to get fairly large portions of it. It was very coarse, and too much upset my stomach, but it contained a lot of the precious vitamin B. Later in Base Camp I had injections made from dudek. It was injected with a blunt needle and as the liquid was very thick it seemed to tear the tissues as it was pushed out of the syringe. It was agony both at the time and for days afterwards, but I had all that could be given to me.

Chapter 26

TROPICAL FLOOD

Life in the forward camp was now approaching a very grim stage. Mac and I bought only the most nourishing food when we had money. We also worked as little as possible to give ourselves a greater chance of survival. If one of us was in camp sick, it was his duty, as soon as he was able to get about, to try to scrounge food to make an extra brew of greens. We used to visit the refuse heaps and sometimes had wonderful finds like pieces of sweet potato peelings that the wealthy Dutch prisoners were able to throw away. Sometimes we would find a few rotting leek tops or a carrot from near the Japanese quarters, and sometimes the cookhouse refuse pile rewarded us with tapioca tops that were considered not worth cooking.

These scrounging journeys about camp often brought other rewards. A rice sack may have been left outside the Japanese cookhouse, and this was a treasure for it could fetch as much as 20 guilders, or about £3. Mac was wonderfully good at raiding from the Japs and once I held my breath when, against my urgent calling to come back, he pinched, in broad daylight, some small, dried salt fish that the Japs laid out in the sun to dry.

On the working parties, too, you had to be quick to take advantage of any opportunity to get extra food. If work stopped near a patch of red ferns we would try to collect enough to take to camp, stripping the tender ones and eating them on the spot. We carried sacking bags which we slung over our shoulders ready to hold anything we could find. We called them squeeze bags. We found that if a native garden was near it paid us to be the first to rush in and grab as much as we could and get back quickly. Always others would follow and, although the Japs would come raging almost immediately, the first in would be able to get some plunder and be back. It was now everyone for himself. The only other person you could worry about was your partner.

Some of the poor natives must have wept when they found their gardens wrecked, though there were few gardens in this deserted place and what we stole was chiefly sweet potato tops. If Mac and I had any money it was the job of the one at work to try to buy tressie and chillies. If our luck was in and we bargained well the price could be lowered to about half of what was the accepted value. This buying was very furtive for both buyer and seller, and done hurriedly, out of sight of any Japs, for if caught both the buyer and the seller were beaten.

When you had completed a purchase satisfactorily there was still the problem of getting it back to camp. Buying from natives was prohibited, and often as we lined up for tenko before going into camp we were searched and any goods confiscated. Sometimes we were made to throw away our pickings of fern leaves, but sometimes the Japs allowed us to keep these.

Stealing was rife by this time and it became more so as our conditions got worse. Fortunately, Mac and I had little of value to anyone else and, after having had my Dutch dixies pinched, I had no worries. I was very disappointed at losing them for I had engraved them with scenes of Haruku and was rather proud of them. But there was nothing else to steal. We had for clothing two G-strings and one sack blanket each. I still had my Australian fur felt hat but Mac had none, and we shared a straw mat which was placed over the planks on our sleeping space. For spoons we each had a piece of aluminium beaten into shape, and for holding our food a half gourd cut longitudinally. For drinking we had a coconut with the top cut off.

When we had our evening wash we washed the G-string that we had worn that day and wore it back to camp wet. At camp we changed to the one that had been hanging to dry and put the wet one in its place. When reveille sounded in the early morning we just got off our beds and were ready for tenko or work. When our food was finished we usually poured most of our tea into the gourd, rinsed it around thoroughly and drank the tea. The gourds were then clean and we hadn't wasted a particle of food.

Our food was poor and inadequate but never again in my life will I enjoy meals more. We relished every grain of rice. If there are compensations in every situation in life, the great enjoyment of the little food that we got was the one compensation in our prison camp life. Food and the anticipation of it was our chief concern, and because of this great urge we forgot other troubles that would have been intolerable if we had been well fed. Every day men with great ulcers on their legs struggled about the small cooking fires making brews, whereas if these same chaps had been as sick at home they would certainly have been bed-ridden and their sore legs the main thought of their lives.

Mac and I welcomed an attack of malaria, for it meant a break off work, but better still it offered a chance, during the first day, of scrounging extra food and making a few needles. Sadly, a dose of malaria which would normally mean weeks in hospital only earned us four or five days off work. The raw cinchona bark rolled into small balls with ongle-ongle was so revolting and upset our stomachs so much that we never took the full amount that we were meant to, and therefore the malaria kept attacking us every few weeks.

Language was quite a feature of our POW life. If any normal, English-speaking person had suddenly found himself in amongst us he would have marvelled at the language, and almost certainly would not have understood half of what was said. It was a mixture of Dutch, Malay, Japanese, American and English. Food was almost universally the Malay word, makan. Sleep or rest was the Jap word, yesame. Often our sentences would have words of half a dozen languages, plus a very good sprinkling of profanity. Most prominent amongst the profanity was the four-letter English word. Dutchmen were always referred to as Honfradomners. This was derived from a Dutch oath which meant "God damn our soul", or something like that. The Malay for Dutchman was Orang Blanda.

I don't think the Japanese thought much of the Dutch. One day a Jap sergeant who was talking to us during our lunch break pointed to the Dutchmen who were eating their meal apart from us and said in Malay, "Dutchmen poor fighter. Australian No.1. Dutchwomen plenty of courage. If Dutch women instead of men had fought for Java, Nippon not able to take." A friend of mine who was working on the Burma Road said that there the Japs had a saying: "One Aussie, fifteen Englishmen, four hundred Dutchmen."

For some months about this time we heard rumours of having to work in a coal mine. We were afraid at the thought of working in a mine, for we could picture the conditions we could expect under Jap administration. A short distance past the station the embankment forked and a branch went off to the right. It was along this branch line that we continued laying rail, and the rumours of a coal mine increased. These rumours were strengthened by the sight of some trucks of coal coming from the direction we were heading toward.

Each day we pushed our rail 2 kilometres further along the line and each day we arrived back at camp later in the day. The monsoon had arrived and the rains came pouring down, but still we worked. We came at last to a wooden bridge across a deep, wide river. It was a very clever piece of engineering to have built such a bridge out in the jungle. The only materials brought from outside the immediate area would have been the iron bolts and spikes. The laying of the tracks across this was very difficult as we had only the sleepers to stand on, and until the rail was spiked they were able to slip about. The river swirled about, 40–50 feet below.

When we had passed the bridge and gone about three days further along the track we knocked off rail-laying and spent a few days ballasting the line, for in places the sleepers had sunk right into the muddy track. One day we were called off work and told to get into the trucks that took us to and from work, and were hurriedly towed along the line towards the bridge. Thunder had been rolling and lightning flashing up country in the hills, and there must have been a cloudburst, for the river, normally swollen at this time, was now almost to the top of the bridge and overflowing its banks. It was an awesome sight, and the roar of the water made it very difficult to hear the orders that were being shouted at us.

A glance at the roaring, yellow river showed that the bridge was in grave danger of being carried away, for a huge dam of logs and driftwood of all kinds had piled up against it. The logs formed a wedge with its apex upstream, and at the bridge almost completely blocked the river. It was only at the two ends of the bridge that the water could pour through, and we found that our job was to get on to the dam and, with long poles, try to manipulate the huge tree trunks as they came floating down, so that they would not add to the accumulation. The party I was with was told to cross almost to the other side of the bridge and then get on to the heaving mass of debris. I was horribly afraid.

In my boyhood in the Bay of Plenty I had seen severe floods, but this one was a far more awesome sight. As we crossed the bridge we could feel it trembling. The logs and debris were covered with a mass of insect life and snakes that had been caught in the flood. I trod on dozens of snakes, and all through the hours I worked on this dam insects were crawling on my body. Sometimes we would not be able to fend off a huge log. Then it would either lodge against the dam and build it further upstream, or it would hit the dam, pause a moment, and then be sucked down to disappear completely or to stay with part of its length poised in the air.

One of the Aussies fell in and was caught by the hand as he disappeared, and hauled out. Once, when I did not hear a Jap shouting at me to do something, he struck me a violent blow on my right ear and knocked me into the water. I was able to grasp a branch and was hauled out, but the blow had damaged my eardrum and left a great throbbing noise in my head.

When night began to fall flares were lit for the work to continue until daylight came. Fearful of work in such a position at night I decided to risk a beat-up, and with a pole on my shoulder as if I had been ordered to the other side I marched boldly across the bridge. When I saw I was not observed I crawled into a native hut and sat in a corner. By this time the night was pitch black and I was not found by the Japs. After about an hour I heard above the tumult of the river two or three loud cracks, like rifle shots. These were followed by a great noise of shouting and the men came rushing back across the bridge. The bridge was breaking. About ten minutes after the warning cracks the three centre pylons were completely carried away and the bridge, held by the rails, bowed downstream and sagged to the torrent.

A crowd of men were marooned on the other side of the river, but miraculously no one was drowned. The truck returned loaded to camp, but as every available man had been rushed to do this job there was not enough room for all, and a small party of us had to remain behind, as did the ones across the river. That night the flood waters rose until all the line except the track near the bridge was under the flood. No trucks could get back for us, so we tried to sleep in the rain, for the small huts were completely flooded. Next day again no trucks managed to get through to us, and it was not until the following evening that we got back to the camp and had some food. We had had nothing to eat for 48 hours. I had an attack of malaria coming on by this time, but much to Mac's disgust I did not leave much of the food that had been saved for me.

When the bridge broke we were overjoyed, for we felt sure that it would be months before any train crossed the river again. But the Japs showed their great power of drive and enterprise, and three days after the rain stopped a train crossed the bridge. We were amazed when we saw how they had shored up the broken span with timber, and after making us all get out of the trucks a Jap drove very slowly across. The bridge still remained bowed downstream and still had its great sag, but the train went across. A large gang of native workmen was employed to repair it.

When we arrived at the finish of the branch line we had laid almost 30 kilometres of track. We found that there was indeed a coal mine there, but it was worked by coolie labour. How many coolies lost their lives in this mine and in making the embankments for the railway I have no idea, but they must have been numbered in thousands.

We spent a further few weeks ballasting this part of the line under very difficult conditions, for it rained every day. Despite the wet and mud the English used to sing when returning to camp in the trucks. This annoyed the Japs and they tried to stop it. Sometimes in the dark, with the rain pouring down, they would stop the train and order all the chaps out to do some unnecessary work. But the singing went on. Time after time on these journeys home the train could not pull up the grades because the wheels were slipping and we would have to get out and push.

I was made the commander of the Aussie hut about this time, and missed the ballasting work on the line to the mines. The job of hut commander was an easy one. After a few weeks, in which I had a good rest, the NCO whom I had replaced because of sickness came back, and I went out to work again. I was lucky to get a job as a water-carrier for the Japanese camp. I had to fill drums with water and heat some of them so that the Japs could have their baths each night. It was hard work, and the day didn't finish until we had washed their dinner dishes. The reward for the job was extra food, for we were able to have the Japs' left-over food, and also got some good opportunities to scavenge cigarette butts. Naturally, I didn't like being the menial of these little men, but when you are hungry and battling to live, feelings don't matter.

Mac was, of course, very glad I had managed to get the job, as each night I would come back with extra rice, and sometimes a lot of fried fish heads which the Japs often left. Usually some of their soup was left and we had that too. I am sure that the extra food gained in this way made a great difference to both Mac and me, and helped us to keep going.

Eventually I had to leave my water-carrying job and go back to rail-laying. By this time the gangs had left the branch line to the mines, and rail had been laid about 20 kilometres further up the main line. Right from the start of the rail job the Japs had spoken of a camp at Logas, where the line was heading, that was going to be paradise. They spoke of running water in the camp and electric light and an abundance of food. About three days after I went back to work on the line we arrived at this paradise. It was a great waste of river-bed which had been gouged out for gold with a large dredge. Electric light ran from somewhere to the idle dredge, and through the area where our camp was being constructed was a stream.

The tempo of the work at this time seemed to have been speeded up, and the tempers of the Japanese were worse. This must have been the beginning of July 1945 and, although we did not know it, the Japs must have realised that they were losing the war. After a period of ballasting the camp moved to Logas, which we called Camp 9.

Chapter 27

BACK TO BASE CAMP

A few days before leaving Camp 8 Mac and I parted. He felt that he could work no longer and though we heard that Base Camp, from where our railway started, was just a death camp, he had the opportunity to get there, and took it. Our parting was quite a break, and in Camp 9 I was a lone ranger.

Camp 9 was no worse than any other camp except in the amount of sleeping space that each man was allowed. The space had been reduced from 39 inches to about 20 inches. You could not sleep on your back, as your shoulders would then crowd the person on either side.

It began to look as though none of the men in Camp 9 could go on much longer. The work had drained most of the chaps' strength and it would not be long before the last of it was gone. On the last days of rail-laying I had noticed the struggle of the rail-carriers to manage the long, heavy rails. It was pitiful to watch them staggering under a weight far greater than they could really manage, but driven on by fear of the Japs. I often hoped that a party of British soldiers would suddenly come upon us as we worked. I pictured their anger at seeing human beings of any kind being treated as we were, and I thought of their added rage when they discovered that these walking skeletons were their own countrymen. I am sure that had this happened not one Jap would have been left alive. I found myself thinking more and more like this, but events didn't happen that way.

I remember one incident that helps to show how fear boosted our strength. I was hancho one day. The work had finished on the line and all that remained was for the bogies to be coupled together and we would go home. One of the bogies was down the bank and we couldn't lift it up. As every minute wasted here delayed our return to camp I asked about eight of the fittest chaps to try to lift it up, but though they tried their hardest they couldn't manage it. The Japanese sergeant who had been watching came over screaming, belted one or two with a stick and then ordered them to lift the bogie on to the line. They did so, apparently quite easily. Most of the time it was fear that drove us on, and it took a great toll on our strength.

The Japanese diesel trucks that pulled these bogies back and forth along the line were wonderfully robust. They worked almost continuously in spite of terrible treatment. Oil was short, and in the end only linseed oil was available. When the engines got hot this oil foamed and poured out of the oil fillers. When working in the garage one day I saw one of the motors stripped down. The crankshaft journals were oval, and I saw a Jap trying to make them round with a rat-tail file, a job normally done with expensive precision equipment.

I worked on rail-laying for about ten days, and then one day I collapsed on the job. Fortunately I was able to stay in the shade beside the track. After work was over I went on sick parade and told the doctor I felt that the same would happen again if I were sent out working and that I had reached the end of my strength. He would not take me off work but sent me out again next day. Again I collapsed after a short time; this time the Jap was angry and I nearly received a beating up for being on the job sick. I reported sick again and this time I was kept in camp. In a few days a draft of sick was sent back to Base Camp and I was amongst them.

It was with mixed feelings that I prepared to leave Camp 9 and go back along the line. The stories of Base Camp were not pleasant. There were stories of huts full of dying men that made me think of the sickness and filth of Haruku. All along the line I felt that I had been through the worst the Japs could possibly offer, but the thought came that perhaps I had been wrong and that Base Camp would be the finish. I was not particularly afraid of death, but I had a great desire to live. At Haruku, for a time I could have died without any regrets, but now after giving fight for all these months I did not want to die. However, rumours were reaching us that things were going well with the war, though we had no sign that this was correct. We occasionally saw a Jap plane but never an Allied one to show us that relief was near.

The steam locomotives had by this time been coming to Camp 9 regularly with loads of rails, and we found out that our journey to Base Camp would be with one of these. A number of empty trucks were being returned, but we were all crowded on to one, and we moved off in the early morning. Not far from the camp we saw an abandoned engine lying on its back with its useless wheels pointing skywards. I wondered if our mild sabotage — the splitting of sleepers — had been the cause, and idly wondered if our train would suffer a similar fate. The speed was so slow that it seemed impossible for any accident to happen other than a derailment, and we were used to these.

Our greatest cause of discomfort was not crowding but sparks from the engine. We had thought that the coal from the mines to which we had built the branch line would have been used in the engines, but they burned wood. Stacks of it were alongside the track at intervals and the engine took on a load of this frequently. The sparks started small fires amongst our kits, and searing pain marked each spot where they landed on our bare skin. But the train steamed on and the journey was interesting, for this was the track we ourselves had made. Our sweat had poured out on to this ground along the entire length from Camp 5 to Camp 9 and memories of all the little daily happenings came flooding back to me.

Here was a patch of red fern in a swamp that had yielded a good picking of soft leaves. There a native garden that we had raided for sweet potato tops, or perhaps a hidden corner where we had contacted a native and bought tressie. Somewhere along the way we crossed the equator. I wondered how many times I had crossed it whilst working. Perhaps I had driven a spike immediately above the calculated line of latitude zero.

Some of this journey back to Base Camp was wonderfully grand, where the giant trees of the jungle raised fluted pillars on either side of the track. I noticed that the jungle had already reclaimed the clearings that we had made, and that the places where the ground had been laid bare to provide soil for the embankment and ballasting were now becoming or had become green; indeed, some of the places we had known so well were now hard to recognise. I tried to find the place that used to be Camp 6, but it was just a wilderness of scrub and I could see no evidence of where it had been. Camp 7 we did see, but only because we knew of its position by the river. Camp 5 still had dilapidated atap huts standing and it looked as if it were occupied, probably by natives. The jungle is sinister in its great fertility. Left for a few months no sign of all our hard work would remain.

We had frequent stops on this journey back over the line but were not allowed out of the truck except when we stopped about midday. Then it was wonderful to relax on the ground and finish our meagre ration of rice, hoping (always vainly) that we would have more food before the day ended.

After we had passed Camp 5 it became dark. I regretted not seeing the country through which we passed for we had only travelled the track once before — the first day after arriving in Pekan Baru on our way to

Camp 5. Later a full moon rose, and in its ghostly light we dimly saw areas of scrub and of jungle. Very occasionally we came to clearings in which a few huts were huddled, but generally it was as desolate an area as the part we had known so well above Camp 5.

About midnight we arrived at Base Camp. Without too much counting we were admitted and an English officer showed us a place to sleep in an atap hut. We were given a quantity of rice and a little stew and thankfully we went to sleep. The journey had taken us from daylight in the morning until midnight, about 18 hours to come about 150 kilometres, or roughly 100 miles.

My first thought on waking was to find Mac and see how he had fared. In the short time we had been in Base Camp Mac had become well known and I had no difficulty in finding him. As usual he had not been too long getting organised and he seemed to be doing fairly well. He had changed in one way, however. I think that the sight of so much sickness in this camp had shocked him, and when we met I saw that the old optimism had vanished, that he was afraid the end to prison camp existence might be in the camp graveyard and not through being released. We could not become partners as before because Mac was now in another section, so I carried on on my own.

For a few days we did no work, but were examined by the doctors. A few of them were old friends from Batavia, for after we had started work others had arrived from Java. One ship had been torpedoed and most of the men lost. I found in Base Camp a number of chaps I had not seen for months or years, and had an interesting time hearing of their movements. Here I learned that the two Vildebeestes which flew from Tasikmalaya Aerodrome a night or so before the Java capitulation had crashed into the sea off the coast of Sumatra as planned, but that the two pilots had difficulty in getting free of the aircraft and had lost their lives. The others had been taken prisoner and remained in Palembang for the duration.

I found that the camp was about half hospital, and that men were dying every day. I don't think the conditions were as bad as Haruku, and that cheered me a lot. I told Mac this too, and assured him that we could last a lot longer if necessary. I think he believed me, and after a while was his optimistic self again.

After a few days of idleness we were all given scabies treatment. This was simple. You had your body smeared with a dirty mixture of old crankcase oil and sulphur. This we left on for 24 hours and then tried to get it off without, of course, any soap. It took days to get clean again. The wash places in Base Camp were very bad and were probably contaminated outside the camp as well as inside. We bathed in large, dirty drains that flowed through the camp. The latrines were good and were constructed on the lower part of the drains just before the water flowed out of camp. The ordure dropped into the water and was carried down the drains. It was primitive but effective. Unfortunately, the same drains had native latrines upstream from us.

In Base Camp I worked in the gardens and occasionally outside the camp, building air raid shelters, for the Japs must have known the end was near. We who had no news but only rumours noted these preparations, but decided they could mean nothing, for in Batavia almost two years before we had built numbers of air raid shelters.

I had one spell in hospital for about a week. I got what I thought was just a more severe attack of my usual malaria. At Base Camp we had better treatment for all complaints and a blood slide was taken. It proved to be malaria but of another sort which, though usually more severe, does not recur. I was not in a part of the hospital kept for the very sick and had quite a good time, as the food was a little better than outside the hospital. I had a sleeping space of about 1 metre.

On one side of me I had a Protestant padre. In the week I was there I could see nothing organically wrong with him, and he went to and from the latrine and moved about outside the hospital freely. I decided he was just living in the hospital because of the extra food and because it gave him an excuse to loaf. All the while he was lying about, the Roman Catholic padre, Father Rorke, was conducting the services and burying all the dead, be they Roman Catholics or Protestants. This loafer lying beside me was fat and, except for the cooks, was one of the fittest men in camp. It disgusted me to see him reverently reading his Bible each night and morning, but what made me more angry was seeing him eat extra food each day with hungry, almost dying, men all about him.

In the camp some of the men made a business of making soup of katyang beans and selling it at a great price to anyone who had money to buy it. Each day this minister of God, who had a captain's rank and therefore money, bought his portion of soup, and often he was the only able-bodied one to do so when the soup came round in the morning. The Roman Catholic priest sold his Bible to be used for cigarette paper and spent the money on the sick. He borrowed money from the officers, and did not repay it, but he spent nothing on himself; it was always for the good of the sick. When I saw him in Base Camp he was as thin as possible and looked like a walking skeleton.

When men died at Base Camp they were wrapped in grass mats and buried in a cemetery in the camp. I am not a Catholic, but I must repeat that of all the padres I met in the prison camps, Padre Rorke was the only one who did his job. The others, as soon as conditions became tough, and even before they became hungry, appeared to think only of preserving their own bodies and not at all of the souls of the men about them.

In a lot of ways our officers also failed to do their jobs. An officer is supposed to put the welfare of his men before his own, and because he is an officer, and is paid at a far higher rate and has great privileges, he is supposed to accept responsibility. In all my work on the rail job the responsibility of being hancho was borne by NCOs, with the exception of the first few days. After that the officers remained in the camp and did camp duties, chiefly in the cookhouse. A great deal of trouble and punishment would have been avoided had there been one officer out at work with us for, though at times the Japs would beat up an officer, they generally respected a commission.

Chapter 28

DAY OF DAYS

One morning at Base Camp came the day of all days, the one we had been waiting for for over three and a half years. We were told by the Japanese that the war was over and that an armistice had been declared. I am a little confused about the sequence of events at this time. I remember that the guards left their posts inside the camp and took them up outside. I remember a little singing and jubilation, but I think we were too overcome to demonstrate very much. I remember quite well that we were still hungry, and in the days that followed our only increase in food was to have the rice ration trebled. This was a very bad thing, for it destroyed the balance of our food, and beriberi increased so alarmingly that the doctors ordered the rice ration to be reduced. I also know that death continued to visit Base Camp as regularly as before, and continued to do so until the doctors had medicine to combat beriberi, dysentery and the tropical ulcers.

The working party up the line returned on August 26 and told how they had been kept working for ten days after the war was over, and that they had joined the line with a section that was being constructed from the other end. When we were in Camp 9 some of the boys reported seeing brass plaques, made in readiness, on which was inscribed: "This line was completed on 24 August, 1945." I did not see the plaques myself, but after hearing the story of how the work was speeded up during the last month and how work went on in shifts during the night I believe that it was a final effort by the Japs to complete the line on the due date regardless of the war finishing and regardless of the amount of life that was lost.

No one knows how many men failed to return to their homes because of that last month of needless toil. The day after the working parties came into Base Camp, I was sent to Camp No. 1, along with a lot of others. Why we were sent I have not the slightest idea. On the day before, we were all issued with a pair of white shorts and a shirt, and when I got to Camp 1 I was one of the first to sell them to the natives and spend the money on food.

TOP RIGHT: 'Mac' in foreground, wearing clothes issued at the end of the war. The 'white socks' are really bandages over leg ulcers.

ABOVE: 'Mac's' camp.

From this time I have only a memory of the main happenings, for events began to crowd upon us rapidly. Wonderful, exciting events. Camp 1 was not a sick camp like Base Camp and to be sent there was a great relief. The showers were better, though the huts were very dilapidated. In Camp 1 I received injections of vitamin B, made in the camp from dudek, or rice polishings. It was wonderful how one of the chemists did this without any proper facilities.

The first big thrill happened soon after we arrived, and I was lucky to be in the camp and take part in it. An aircraft from Ceylon dropped parachute packages to us. This was the first indication that our position was known and that we were not a lost battalion, as was rumoured in the camp. Along with all the other boys I cheered and cheered and quite unashamedly cried for joy as the large aircraft displaying the roundels of the R.A.F. circled around us and then, coming in low, dropped the first of the packages. Unfortunately, of the first eight dropped, six went into the deep river and though five were fished out after great effort, the contents were wet. In the next run in the drop landed accurately. Of course we only had a share of the drop on Camp 1 and there were not enough articles to go around, but we at Camp 1 did have the privilege of being the first to know that we were not forgotten.

We had all hoped for food. Food had been our chief thought for years, and still was. We were disappointed to find that the drop was of toilet articles and a few cigarettes, a great number of which were soaked in the river. The things dropped were not enough to go around and were balloted for. I was lucky to receive a cloth bag with shaving soap and facecloth. I still have the bag at home. Each person in the camp had ten cigarettes. Some were wet, but what a joy they were!

A few days after the drop three of us sneaked out of the camp after dark. I am a bit hazy about this adventure but I know we considered it quite a risky thing to do, probably because the Japs were still guarding the outside of the camp. Why we were guarded thus, after the war was over, I do not know, unless it was because the natives were in a bad condition and might have attacked us, or else because the authorities thought that many would lose their lives if they were allowed freedom in this area. At any rate I remember that we took the strictest precautions not to be caught as we left camp, and sneaked through a patch of jungle to buy a cup of coffee and cakes from the native shop. I was feeling ill with another dose of malaria coming on but I remember the thrill of tasting the sweet black coffee.

We got back to camp without any incident, but I found as soon as I got into my hut that an ambulance had arrived in camp and that they had been searching for Sergeant Thompson all over camp. No one knew why, and I could think of nothing I had done. Before I had time to find the answer the driver of the ambulance again came into the hut and told me I had to pack my gear and come with him.

"Where the hell to?" I asked.

"Search me," he replied. So with no inkling of why I was wanted and amidst farewells from the chaps in the hut I got into the ambulance and was driven away.

After the Japs had announced that the war was over the senior officer, an English Wing Commander, moved out of Base and set up a headquarters camp a short distance away. From here he organised the feeding of the camps. He took over from the Japs a considerable number of trucks which, driven by the British boys, collected the rations, etc. My destination in the ambulance was headquarters camp where I was given a place to sleep and then told that the Wing Commander wanted to see me. It was then about midnight. The Wing Commander had been in 100 Squadron before the war and because of that we had had a few chats about the squadron, but I did not know him well. When I saw him this night he told me that he had a special job for me. He wanted a pilot to take a small party out to an aerodrome about 7 kilometres away to inspect a suitable runway and to light smoke fires if aircraft approached so that they would know the surface wind. He told me to take five other air force boys with me and that we could live in a permanent building on the drome that had formerly been the waiting room. Our rations, he said, would be sent out each day. I said, "Thank you, sir. I will enjoy doing it", and left him.

My mind just leaped at this break. At the aerodrome we would be under no control and could trade with natives. We would be the first to meet any planes. What a glorious chance for a wonderful change, if I had the right chaps with me. Mac, unfortunately, was out, for he was not air force. Mentally I searched amongst my friends to pick those who knew the rackets, and were game enough to scrounge and get things done, but would still carry out orders. About 1 a.m. I found out the sleeping place of one Tommy Pursglove and, waking him, said, "What about coming with me on a good thing?"

"What?" he said.

"I have to take five boys with me and stay in the aerodrome. We should be able to live like kings out there."

"Christ, yes. Can my mate come too?"

"Yes, but we have to find three others who will all muck in together and there will be work, you know. I would like Blondy to come. So that leaves two more."

In a short time we arranged with the others and I went to bed, cursing a bad attack of malaria that was again burning me up. I did not sleep, my mind was too active. I had a crowd of chaps that I knew would be the right types for the job. They were all fellows who would get the work done first. They all knew how to look after themselves. In fact, they were great racketeers. It now seems unfair that when these good jobs came along with a chance of better conditions it was usually the ones that could look after themselves that got them.

Tommy and his friends had been working on the trucks and knew their way about. Before I left him he told me he knew that Jap overalls had been found in a godown (warehouse) and a lot of them had been brought into camp. He suggested that I try to get a set each from the Wing Commander. This was a splendid scheme; they should be worth about 400 guilders each. Next morning I managed to get two pairs of overalls each. I also arranged that a sack of rice would be included in our gear, and off we went by truck to the aerodrome.

We found that the Japs had been living in our building but were moving out when we arrived. They had organised a number of natives to work for them as servants and we took these over to work for us. Quickly we set about our plans and soon, by selling a few overalls, had plenty of money. Tommy was a good cook, and was put in charge of the cookhouse and the native cook. The others just made themselves comfortable and bought food.

For years all our thoughts had been about food and we had pictured great bunches of bananas ripening, while our mouths had watered at the very thought of meat, chicken and eggs. That afternoon all this became reality. With rice and money, in a few hours we had the hut festooned with bunches of bananas. The Japs had kept chickens, and the coops that were empty when we arrived were soon full.

For lunch we had rations sent from camp but from then on until we left we lived in luxury. The luxury was more than the food; our quarters were comfortable and the Japs had left mattresses behind. We left them in the sun and then used our grass mats on them as sheets. We soon had two native boys whose job it was to heat water for our baths. On the drome there were some wrecked Jap transport planes, and we had the natives dig the nose cap of one of these into the ground to be used as a bath. But we did not neglect work. Soon we had a runway roughly marked out; we made the native boys build stacks of timber ready to be lit quickly and beside these we had green material to be thrown on to make a good smoke.

These days we spent on the aerodrome were probably the most exciting I shall ever spend. Because of that, and the fact that I was really sick and should have been in bed but was too excited to stay there, I am a little confused about the number of days we were there before greater events began to happen. But one day as we were sitting at our table eating another enormous meal we heard our first plane. In a few moments we had the fires lit and we waved frantically as an R.A.F. Liberator flew low over the drome and then circled away to make a run in, we thought to drop supplies. With a mighty roar this large plane came in low and suddenly from it tumbled six packages. This was what we were there for. We started to rush towards where they would land but stopped in amazement. The bundles swinging from the white canopies were men. We just went mad then and each made for a different man as we raced across the drome towards them. How I got the strength to run as I did I don't know, but I made the long distance across the drome in marvellous time.

Before we reached them the men had landed and, not knowing what kind of creatures were racing towards them, prepared for action; they lay flat on the ground with weapons ready. Before I reached my man he must have realised that the strange, almost naked, browned and bearded creature was no enemy and, rising, came forward to greet me. I shall never forget his greeting. It was far better than the classical: "Dr. Livingstone I presume?" He said very politely with his hand extended, "How do you do? My name is Barclay, Dr. Barclay."

Probably my reply was quite incoherent but I am sure he understood. He was a fine man. Collecting his parachute we returned to the building. The others came, too, and I found that most of them had been armed with tommy guns and that they had been briefed in Ceylon to expect possible hostile action from both the natives and the Japanese. The party of six comprised the doctor, his orderly, an Australian who was an interpreter, an R.A.F. radio officer and two others that I remember little about. The only casualty was the orderly, who had a sprained ankle. What a joy it was to entertain these men and give them a meal. I am sure that after that meal they could not have thought too badly of the Jap POW diet. In fact, they mentioned that food seemed plentiful, but our explanation would have been proved true when they went into the camps afterwards.

The plane had been seen in the main camp and soon a truck was out to pick up supplies. The Wing Commander was out, too, and was as amazed as we were that parachutists had come. Two packages had been dropped; they contained medicinal supplies.

The R.A.F. officer stayed out with us and we had a great evening. In a few hours we learned the war news of three and a half years. The following day we were again visited by a plane which dropped a radio set for our guest and also a container of food for his personal use. He put this into our stores and for the first time we had normal European food included in our diet. The Wing Commander was now often out at mealtimes for we were undoubtedly the best fed people in Sumatra at that time.

How many days it was before the planes landed I am not sure. I was still very sick, but was too excited to go to bed for long. I remember that during this time a Japanese plane arrived. It was a small one and carried a pilot and a high-ranking Jap officer. I remember the delight with which we refused to allow the plane to be refuelled, making the Jap officer wait about. After an hour we sent him into the camp to see the Wing Commander. When he arrived there the interpreter found out about him. It turned out that he was a V.I.P. of some sort and was on a very urgent mission so we let him go on his way.

One afternoon we heard planes approaching and rushed out to light our fires. Three planes approached and were ready for a drop. Instead, however, they landed and turned out to be three Australian Dakotas. It was wonderful greeting the crew, but most wonderful of all was the sight of an Australian nursing sister. For years we had seen only an occasional native woman, and to see again one of our own kind was sheer joy.

One of the Aussies gave Dr. Barclay a bottle of Australian beer. The doctor gave it to me and I shared it with the others of our party. I thought before I tasted it that perhaps it would have lost its attraction, but my first sip assured me that it was still the same. It was a great treat and was probably the only bottle of beer drunk in Sumatra that day.

Unlike the packages dropped at Camp 1 the cargo of the Aussie planes was all food. The Wing Commander was out soon after they arrived, and he organised the truck and some Indian soldiers to take the food to camp. The planes flew back that afternoon with only one passenger, an Australian who had a tumour on the brain and had to be operated on urgently. I think the pilots were a bit afraid of the aerodrome and that is why they flew back empty.

Exciting events crowded the following day. The first was the arrival of a shiny, glistening Dakota that looked very smart compared with the drab camouflaged ones we had seen the day before. It, too, landed, and its passenger was Lady Louis Mountbatten. What she thought of us in our almost naked state I do not know, but I formed the highest opinion of her. She went almost immediately into the camps and inspected them thoroughly. She even went through all the dysentery huts, a thing that we, hardened to the conditions, could hardly bear to do. The pilot of Lady Mountbatten's plane was very friendly towards me and we had some good talks.

About two hours after the arrival of Lady Mountbatten's plane the three Aussie planes returned, again full of food. This time they stayed the night and the crew stayed with us at the drome. Being a Kiwi I was like a relative of the Aussies so I asked them if they would take me and the other New Zealanders out when they went back. I had a lot in common with these aircrew chaps and they agreed that, unless ordered otherwise, they would take us all back if I got the New Zealand boys out to the drome. I was assured by the pilot of Lady Mountbatten's plane that he would see that I got back with him if the Aussies could not manage it.

I had asked an Aussie radio operator on the previous visit if he could send a signal to my home in New Zealand and he said he would. On this visit he told me that the signal had been sent and that my folks at home should now know I was alive and safe. It was a very wonderful evening for us, and we talked late into the night.

To make sure that the New Zealand boys got out in time I had to make an early start. I had to ride to the camp in a truck, locate the other New Zealanders and tell them to get out quickly to the aerodrome. There were numbers of trucks on the road by then and the boys easily found lifts. One boy was going to be sent out in any case and travelled by ambulance. I found Mac, doing well for himself, as I had expected. Somehow he had managed to get into the camp canteen and was doing very well indeed, though his standard of living wasn't up to ours. I told him to jump the first truck he could and get out to the aerodrome. There were only five New Zealanders apart from myself and they all got out in plenty of time. I was the only one who nearly missed; I just caught the last plane as it taxied out to the runway. I should have liked to say goodbye to my friends but could only give them a hasty wave as I rushed to the plane.

Inside we sat on the floor and were allowed to smoke. In about two hours we landed at Singapore and girls in uniform gave us cups of tea.

Soon we had left Kalang Aerodrome and were at a large Australian general hospital. Here an Aussie corporal tried to turn the six New Zealanders away, allowing only the Aussies that had come with us to be admitted. But after a while we proved our point that we were next door to Aussies and that anyhow there were only six of us, so he let us in. Our clothes were taken from us and we were covered in D.D.T. powder. By this time, due to lack of sleep, to excitement, and to malaria, I was just about in a state of collapse, and was most thankful to be taken upstairs along with the others and put to bed.

It is impossible to describe my feelings when we were put to bed and efficient, good-looking nurses took charge. The change from squalor had been too abrupt and tears came flooding to my eyes whenever one of the nurses did anything for me. To have been just given sheets and a bed would have been luxury indeed, but to have all our needs looked after by these nurses was something I shall never forget. To be treated once again as a civilised human being was just too much to take.

For a week I was kept in bed while the malaria burned itself out. Each day I received a great handful of pills and had injections of vitamins. The food was good, too, but we never had enough, for they feared too much would be harmful. It did little good to tell the sister that I had eaten hearty meals for some days before coming to hospital. After a week in bed I was allowed up for short periods and in these times I was sent to see different specialists and was X-rayed for T.B., but it proved to be negative. To me it was amazing that this great hospital with its eye, ear and throat specialists, X-ray equipment and about 600 beds, had been established in only three days. I found I was far luckier than some and that my eyesight, though bad, had not deteriorated beyond recovery point. Some poor chaps' eyes would never recover.

Mac and I left on almost the last plane to New Zealand, and we left with three kitbags each. We were desperately keen to get possessions and took anything that we could get from the quartermaster's store. Most of the good stuff such as shirts and shorts had been taken by others leaving before us, but in typical army fashion the last plane to arrive from New Zealand had almost a complete load of service boots and socks. I got seven pairs of boots. We also had quite a number of sets of woollen underwear. Between Singapore and Australia I visited the quartermaster's stores and got more gear and more kitbags.

Many people experience the thrill of seeing the long thin outline of New Zealand appear, but few will have seen it with as much pleasure as

Mac and I. In Singapore, Mac had received cables and letters and knew how things were with the family, but though I had sent many messages I had received no news from home and I wondered what I would find. In fact, my mother was waiting at the airport to greet me. She had sent letters and cables but they must have been lost or given to the wrong person. She was fit and well, and it was good to see her again. Like other mothers she had suffered greatly through not knowing whether I was alive or dead.

EPILOGUE

I feel I have gained immeasurably because of my experience during those three and a half years of imprisonment. I had a wealth of human experience that is fortunately not the lot of many, but now that I have come through it and am reasonably well I am thankful.

I find now that I do not hate Japs because they are Japs. I hate a number of individuals who beat me up. I hate some of their leaders and I hate the system that made the Japs act as they did. They treated us as slaves, but they also treated their own soldiers very badly. I wonder how I would have acted if I had been born Japanese, and had had to grow up in Japanese surroundings. I would have found, I am sure, that life was held very cheaply in that crowded country.

I am not condemning the actions of the Japanese. They killed thousands of soldiers quite unnecessarily, but no one knows what their reactions would have been had they had the same advantages that we of the Western world have enjoyed.

* * *

I want to write about hunger; not the hunger you feel when you have missed one meal or two, or maybe a day's meals or a week's meals, but the hunger that comes after months and months of not having enough food to sustain the body, so that hunger becomes a great driving force in ones life. It is so strong that eating habits go by the board, and you tend to become like a ravenous animal. Because of our conditions on the railway we had got down again to being starved and having a great craving for food, immediate food, food to put into our bellys and give us something to digest. We were very sick, but sickness became a secondary thing to the drive for food. Food that was dropped on the ground and was in filthy condition was eaten without any qualms whatsoever. The craving for food was so strong that it superseded all the rules of hygiene we had been taught before.

One camp I was in was not far from the equator. It was a camp like others on the railway line, with no barbed wire. Beside the line a clearing had been carved out of the jungle and our huts were built on this. Japanese sentries had a hut from which they could see a long distance along the track each way. The main guard quarters were in the centre of the camp. After rain at night we could see, in the mud outside the camp, the tracks of all sorts of animals including tigers — and Sumatran tigers are the largest of them all. The Japanese were terrified of the tigers, and always had a large fire blazing at night. After our evening meal a sergeant came out with a bucket full of the scrapings from plates from their mess. He took great pleasure demeaning the POWs by beating the bucket with a spoon as a farmer would for his animals and seeing the scramble of lot of the POWs getting a measure of the awful mess — there were always takers. One day this changed when the sergeant got a pig. We hated that pig, and hated it more as the sergeant gloatingly watched it fatten day by day. At night sleep was often broken by the guards imagining a tiger was in the camp. To be awakened so suddenly by shooting or by some POW having a shocking nightmare caused me, as I wakened, to see into the abyss of horror and terror. That is, I believe, often the lot of alcoholics with the DTs. It was only for a moment but awful. Still, the pig thrived and the sergeant gloated. We hated that pig!

One night all hell broke loose. The Japanese were screaming and firing shots all over the place, and above all this was a high-pitched squeal. We kept as quiet as possible. I had my moments of horror and fear. Only the two POWs at the end of the hut could see what was happening. Slowly the message came back. Relax, a tiger has pinched the pig!

* * *

I have a theory that it is normal one tends to forget the bad things that happen to one quite quickly, and remember only the good. This has been my experience.

After I came home to New Zealand I went through a long period of almost continuous ill health. I was in a hospital in Market Road, Remuera, for a long time. There, I was filled up with vitamins for my beriberi and scurvy, and went on a long course of anti-malarial treatment and, when I was fit enough, had hookworm treatment. It was not completely successful, and I was sent home to the Bay of Plenty to recover, only to have it occur again. Eventually I was discharged, but I suffered continual illness. I had a long bout of boils and carbuncles, recurring bronchitis and malaria, a serious kidney operation for a very large stone, and frequent stomach trouble. I remember little of this long period except the kindness of the people who took an interest in me, visited me in hospital, and when possible took me to their homes for short visits and then to stay for longer visits. Mac's wife and sister-in-law had a home in Portland Road, not far from the hospital, and it became a home for me, too.

Eventually I was well enough to work. I became a life insurance salesman. I did quite well at this job, but I hated it. I dressed well and had a Vauxhall car, but I was having to go to see my doctor a great deal. On one of these visits he said, "Claude, I know you don't like selling life insurance, but you are doing well at your job, so you must not give it up. You must, however, do more work with your hands. I suggest that you buy an old boat or an old house and spend all your spare time using your hands." I had a land agent friend, and through him bought a two-storied old house in awful condition situated beside the Auckland Gas Works. All my friends thought I was crazy. I thought so myself at times. It was cheap, however, and with no experience of building I started. I made a lot of mistakes, but I kept on at it.

The first part I completed was the small self-contained flat for myself, and I moved in. I became a good rough cook and had friends around at times. My day started early, usually in the dark. I had a good breakfast and worked on the building until I had just time to have a shower, get dressed for the city and be at work at 9.00 a.m. My flat was in the bottom part of the house; I could drive to the back of the house and have good parking. The section was a steep one and the entrance to the top floor was quite separate. One morning I finished work at the top entrance and was just going to have my shower when the postman came past. He was a cheery person and said, "You're brightening up the old house, it looks good. Do you own it?" I said, "Yes, it's taking a lot of work, but I will get it finished one day." I had a quick shower, dressed and went out to my letter box. The cheery postman was returning. He said, "The old house looks good, it's a lot brighter." I said, "I will get it finished eventually, it's taking more time than I thought." He said, "Do you own it?" I told him I did. "That's funny," he said, "a scruffy old bugger up top said he owned it," and he went away shaking his head.

I had been asked to a luncheon by the Auckland Chamber of Commerce, and became a member. I found it a stimulating organisation. After a while I was too old for the Juniors and became a member of the

Intermediate Section of the Senior Chamber. I found working with these bright young businessmen very rewarding. We had marvellous relaxation weekends as well.

Before I could finish my building work I ran out of money. This was big trouble. An old friend came to see how I was getting on and I told him I would have to get a job to make some extra cash. He took me to see a chap who had some gangs spraying D.D.T. in houses, so I became a sprayer. Each gang had a salesman, a sprayer, and a boss to organise and supply the plant and materials. From the price charged the boss took 25 per cent for material and plant, 25 per cent for organising and I got 25 per cent as did the salesman. I had a good salesman so I had plenty of work. I started about the end of November and worked over Christmas until the end of January, and made enough money to finish the flats I was building and get them tenanted. I then made a trip to Gisborne and became engaged. This was the best thing I ever did. Betty, who became my wife in May, was happy to share my small flat and she made it a home, a very happy one in all ways. Eighteen months later Peter, our first child, was born while we were still in the flat. I made a small bedroom for him; he was a joy.

My priority at Rehabilitation was very high. When our second child was on its way I decided to get a Re-Hab loan. We selected a good section at Kohimarama and I went to see Re-Hab. At first my interview went very well. However, when I had to answer a question about property and I told of my old building I was again in trouble. In vain I argued that I shouldn't be penalised because I had made a small income for myself. I told them it was a lifeline to me as I was still frequently sick. They were adamant, and I was turned down. Amongst my friends who applied for loans I am the only one that I know of who did not get a loan, not even a furniture loan. It was a great blow. With hindsight, though, it was one of the best things that happened to me. To get suitable housing we had to buy something old and very cheap. We bought two houses on one section. They could not be subdivided. One was tenanted at 15/- a week rent and the other was empty. I worked like a slave to get this one fit for my family and made a very comfortable home. We had a harbour view and a very sunny position. Simon, our second son, was born after we moved in. After a while our tenants moved out and I made this house into two flats. I bought another old wreck of a house in Parnell and made flats there. We had decided that as soon as possible we would leave the city and live in the country. We chose Warkworth, a delightful small town about 40 miles north of Auckland, as the most desirable place. It took us a few years to get there but eventually we were able to leave. Once more, it had to be old and cheap, but again I was able to make a comfortable home. We brought a charming daughter Elizabeth with us, and in Warkworth a third son, James, was born.

I had bought the D.D.T. company I had worked for as a sprayer, and built up a seasonal job spraying D.D.T. The income from this and the rents from the flats were just sufficient to allow us to move to Warkworth. In Warkworth I became a land agent. I kept spraying D.D.T. for about two months each year for about 20 years. I love old houses and have had to spray some of the loveliest old homes in New Zealand. That was the bonus for a lot of hard work.

We are still in Warkworth as I write this, and there is no place I would rather live in. An old house that we had coveted, but was not for sale for years, is now our home.

Looking back, the things that helped me most to rehabilitate myself were my wife Betty, my doctor's advice, the refusal of Re-Hab to give me a loan and the wonderful friends who helped me. The greatest of these friends was the poet Rex Fairburn, who, over many years prior to his premature death in 1957, had a deep-felt affinity with the area which was to become our lasting home. Rex had, in fact, written a poem in 1946 which encapsulates much of my own feelings about the recuperative strengths and properties of my final resting place. It reads:

AWAY FROM IT ALL

All I ask is a minimum of commotion,
and an unimpeded view of the Pacific Ocean.

I'll need a good store of some old-time potion
— say bottled Guiness. Skip the sunburn lotion.

I want to sail boats like a Nova Scotian,
and to follow the tides with a dog-like devotion.

I want to leave behind me all rancid emotion.
I want to be alone. I want to forget Goschen.

I want to lie still, and feel the earth's motion,
with nothing in my head, not a whim or a notion.

I feel that I have had a very good life and that fate has been very kind. I have a feeling that it has looked after me. I am religious in an unconventional way. I love nature and its beauty. I am amazed at the perfection of the human body and its power to recuperate from illness, damage and hard work. I am awed with the size and grandeur of the universe.

Sir James Jeans, a famous astronomer, when describing the size of the universe said that the ratio of our sun to all other suns was of the order of one grain of sand to all the grains of sand on all the beaches of the world. I know my place.